Fight the Good Fight of Faith

PREVIOUSLY PUBLISHED WITH RESOURCE PUBLICATIONS

Nonfiction

Storms Are Faith's Workout: Preparing Christians for Spiritual Ambush (2018).
Faith's Journey Confronts Obstacles: Instructing God's Soldiers to Overcome in his Armor (2019).
Satan's Strategy to Torment Through Physical Ambush: Educating God's Soldiers of Satan's Plot to Shatter Faith through Sickness and Disease (2019).
Spiritual Shipwreck on the Horizon: Exhorting Christians to Contend for the Faith and Comprehend the Deceitfulness of Sin (2019).
Satan Has No Authority Over God's Soldier: Illuminating Godlike Faith (2019).
God The Holy Spirit: The Conquering Power Within (2019).
Signs of the Time: Warning: Lukewarm Christianity Accepts Deception (2020).
Flesh and Spirit Conflict: The Inner Battle of Choice (2020).
Supernatural Faith Disables: Quench the Fiery Darts (2020).
Seeds of Knowledge: Soil Determines The Seed's Harvest (2020).
An Incorruptible Crown: Perseverance Conquers All Impediments (2021).

Fiction

The Elfdins and the Gold Temple: An Oralee Chronicle (2018).
Charlie McGee and the Leprechaun: Life's Curious Twist of Events (2019).
The Shrines of Manitoba: Dark Secrets Shall Be Brought to Light (2019).
Guilty as Blood: One Can Make A Difference (2019).
Back From The Dead: Light Shines as the Noonday Sun (2020).
Nazis, Holocaust, and Self-Love: Unbridled Bigotry (2020).
Chateau de Paix: Nightmare Hiding In Paradise (2020).
The Elfdins and the Gold Cross: An Oralee Chronicle: Book 2 (2021).

Fight the Good Fight of Faith

Run the Race with Patience

R. C. JETTE

RESOURCE *Publications* • Eugene, Oregon

FIGHT THE GOOD FIGHT OF FAITH
Run the Race with Patience

Copyright © 2021 R. C. Jette. All rights reserved. Except for brief quotations in critical publications or reviews, no part of this book may be reproduced in any manner without prior written permission from the publisher. Write: Permissions, Wipf and Stock Publishers, 199 W. 8th Ave., Suite 3, Eugene, OR 97401.

Resource Publications
An Imprint of Wipf and Stock Publishers
199 W. 8th Ave., Suite 3
Eugene, OR 97401

www.wipfandstock.com

PAPERBACK ISBN: 978-1-6667-3303-7
HARDCOVER ISBN: 978-1-6667-2728-9
EBOOK ISBN: 978-1-6667-2729-6

10/01/21

All Scripture references are taken from the KING JAMES VERSION (KJV): KING JAMES VERSION, public domain.

This book is dedicated to my Lord Jesus Christ in whom I live and move and have my being.

To my husband (Paul) who is my comrade-in-arms.

My daughter (Dawn) to whom words cannot convey my love and gratitude.

My daughter (Christina), my son (PJ), my grandchildren (Andrew, Matthew, Joshua, Kierra), and granddaughter Sarah who is with the Lord), my cousins (Mike and Susanna).

I give heartfelt thanks to all who have helped me on my journey to that city which hath foundations whose builder and maker is God.

My special thanks is given to Wipf and Stock Publishers for their continued publication of my books under their Resource Publications.

I am grateful to Joe Delahanty, Jim Tedrick, Ian Creeger, Kara Barlow, Stephanie Randels, Jonathan Hill, and Rachel Saunders.

Special mention must be given to Matthew Wimer, George Callihan, Shannon Carter, and Savanah N. Landerholm for their incredible assistance.

Fight the good fight of faith, lay hold on eternal life, whereunto thou art also called, and hast professed a good profession before many witnesses.

—1 Timothy 6:12

Wherefore seeing we also are compassed about with so great a cloud of witnesses, let us lay aside every weight, and the sin which doth so easily beset us, and let us run with patience the race that is set before us.

—Hebrews 12:1

Contents

Introduction		ix
Chapter 1	Choose Whom You Serve	1
Chapter 2	Press Forward	8
Chapter 3	Look Up For Help	14
Chapter 4	Other Gods	23
Chapter 5	Spiritual Authority	30
Chapter 6	Apathetic Indifference	39
Chapter 7	Walk in the Spirit	47
Chapter 8	Suffering And Gethsemane	52
Chapter 9	Champion Runner	60
Chapter 10	Spiritual Seeker	65
Chapter 11	No Distractions	71
Chapter 12	Aggressive Warfare	76

Introduction

THIS BOOK IS MEANT to encourage God's soldiers to commit our lives once again to overcoming all barriers through diligently fighting the good fight of faith and running the race set before us with steadfast patience. To bring forth the necessity of resoluteness, I will, as done a few times in the past, borrow precise information from my previous books to help enlighten our insight. Sometimes repetition brought forth through a different approach or in a new light can birth a revelation not heretofore grasped.

There is much distraction in this world and many have lost sight of our race and turned our attention towards this life. We are living in the now instead of focusing upon our future inheritance. It is imperative for us to realign our focus from the present to eternity. The necessity to fight the good fight of faith and run the race set before us with patience or tenacity cannot be overemphasized. In this day and time of itching ears preaching that has caused some to meander onto the broad and wide path, this truth must be addressed without ceasing.

We must fight the desires of our flesh and worldly attractions. If not, we will be enticed to listen to those preaching messages that there is no need to deny self. False teachers instruct that once saved, we can indulge in any sinful behavior because Jesus took all our sins. Yet, Jesus made clear that unless we are denying self, taking up our cross daily, we are not following him.

Fight the Good Fight of Faith

To fight means to take part in a violent struggle. Unless we are willing to battle our flesh to conquer all that is contrary to the will of God, we will stay focused upon this life. As God's soldiers, it is our lot to fight daily battles as sure as the sun rises and sets each day. Only through fully comprehending that we are soldiers or warriors for the Lord will we fight whatever we face each day. When we accepted Jesus as savior, we signed up as soldiers in the army of the Lord for life. Our obligation ends when we take our last breath.

Our faith journey is not a skip through the park, it is a journey full of sufferings, battles, hurdles, winding turns, thorns, hardships, struggles, grief, etc. that must be fought daily. It is a race that without unrelenting faith, we will not be empowered to run with patience.

It seems many of God's soldiers are overwhelmed with the battles to be fought day in and day out. We feel as though we are getting nowhere and think there is no light at the end of the tunnel. We have become weary of the long arduous race set before us, the restrictions upon our flesh, the pull to go back to Egypt or our old life, and the desire to join those on the broad and wide way. We want to have life easier and want to quit the fight of faith. We are becoming weary of the never-ending struggles.

We have forgotten all who live godly in Christ Jesus will suffer persecution (2 Timothy 3:12). We have forgotten if they persecuted Jesus, his servants will also be persecuted (John 15:20). We have forgotten without opposing our old nature, we will not continue to fight our flesh and its affinity to sin (Galatians 5:17).

We forgot we joined the army of the Lord for life. We forgot this life is about to become a vapor (James 4:14). It will all vanish away and what will our life have wrought? Will we have sold our birthright for a morsel of meat or some fleshly desire (Hebrews 12:16)? Will we have quit fighting? Will we have abandoned the race?

If we forget Satan has no authority over us, he will take what is not his to take. He has no power to subdue us, unless we submit to him through sin, unbelief, worry, fear, etc. Christ has conquered Satan and has given us the same authority and power to

Introduction

do likewise. Faith is the victory that enables us to overcome any hurdle we may have to encounter.

Only persevering in fighting the good fight of faith or running with patience will prevent us from being seduced by the temptations of this world. The seduction is like a drip of water that keeps dripping until it becomes a puddle, then a pool, then a pond, then a lake, then an ocean.

Leaven starts off microscopic, like malignancy, until it has leavened or corrupted the whole. If we allow a little lethargy, compromise, or seduction in our life, we will be overcome by sin. Once that occurs, we will have lost sight of eternity and no longer fight the good fight of faith.

I pray if you have picked up this book, it will be the nugget you need to live a life of victorious faith. Although you have read other books on faith, you do not yet comprehend how to fight the good fight of faith. Allow the Holy Spirit to open your eyes of enlightenment and reveal how to run your race with resolute endurance until you cross the finish line!

Chapter 1

Choose Whom You Serve

And if it seem evil unto you to serve the Lord, choose you this day whom ye will serve; whether the gods which your fathers served that were on the other side of the (flood), or the gods of the Amorites, in whose land ye dwell; but as for me and my house, we will serve the Lord. (Joshua 24:15)

WITHOUT DECIDING WHO WE will serve, there is no fighting the good fight of faith nor running the race set before us with patience. The verse in Joshua tells us to choose. It is a choice which we make and no other can make it for us. We must select, decide upon, or determine who we will serve.

That choice or decision determines every other choice we make in life. What we choose to serve is the foundation upon which the rest of our life is built upon and determines our eternal destination. If we choose God, our life will be built upon faith, righteousness, holiness, godliness. If we choose self or false gods, our life will be built upon unbelief, unrighteousness, unholiness, ungodliness.

It is important to comprehend we may say we have made the choice to serve God, but when faced with hurdles of sufferings, storms, obstacles, trials, grief, difficult times, we can waiver like a reed tossed in the wind. Our decision was not sure and certain. It is easy to say something or commit to something when the choice is not under attack, assault, or persecution.

We can never fight the good fight of faith unless our choice to serve God is steadfast, unmoveable, always abounding in the work of the Lord, for our labor is not in vain (1 Corinthians 15:58). We alone choose to live for this life or to live for eternity. As we persevere in fighting the good fight of faith and running the race with patience, we will be prevented from being seduced by the temptations that could cause us to forget eternity and live for this life.

I know there are so many books out there about faith. However I believe whenever we see things from a different perspective, it can cause the lightbulb of revelation to turn on. If we are to overcome by faith, we must be prepared for spiritual warfare. Only the never surrender mentality will enable us to fight the good fight of faith and finish our race with patience.

In our society of instant this and instant that, Christians can be swayed into the mentality of not enduring, fighting, or persevering until the fight is won or the race is finished. Faith is not always understood. Like I stated in my introduction, sometimes seeing something from a different perspective can clarify what was not understood before.

This book is to reveal that to live in victorious faith, we must first be prepared for spiritual warfare and fight the good fight of faith until we win our race. All the struggles we confront in this life can be a hindrance. If we are not willing to fight for our faith, it will obstruct the race set before us.

> *Thus saith the Lord, thy Redeemer, the Holy One of Israel; I am the Lord thy God which teacheth thee to profit, which leadeth thee by the way that thou shouldest go. (Isaiah 48:17)*

God promises to teach (guide, instruct) us to profit (benefit, advance) while He leads (directs, shepherds) us in the way (the path, the course of life) we are to go.

Isaiah promises God will guide us so that we profit. He is assuring us that we will benefit, be profitable if He is guiding us. He pledges to lead us into what will profit us. When we allow him to guide us, He will help us to know what we should say, what we should do, what course of action we should take, what direction we should go in, and whether we should or should not do or say something.

> 5)Trust in the Lord with all thine heart; and lean not unto thine own understanding. 6)In all thy ways acknowledge him, and he shall direct thy paths. (Proverbs 3:5-6)

In all our ways (all modes of action or conversation), we must acknowledge (yield) to him, and He shall direct (guide) our paths (which direction) to take.

What does this imply? It indicates that if we are to profit, He must be the one leading or guiding our life. Without him leading us, we will not know how to fight the good fight of faith or how to avoid the hurdles that can hinder us from running our race. If we are to be led by God, logic or our own understanding must take a back seat in Christianity. Man's logic, intellect is not rooted in faith. It is not based upon God's power and ability, but man's power and ability. Our thoughts and ways are not his thoughts and ways. For as the heavens are higher than the earth, so are his thoughts and ways compared to our thoughts and ways (Isaiah 55:8-9).

He knows we can choose not to follow him or not to be led by him because of our own will, our own understanding. Our logic, our education, our understanding, our feelings, our training, our beliefs can get in the way. If any of these hinder us, there is no fight of faith and no running our race to finish our course. If we choose to serve anything other than God, we will not profit.

The title of this chapter reveals that we must choose whom we will serve. That choice will be the groundwork of our life. If we do not choose to serve God, there will be no salvation. Without a salvation experience, there is no new birth or being born again. Without being born again, there is no fight of faith and no race to run. Only those who walk by faith will overcome this life and inherit all things with Christ. The inheritance of those who do not choose to serve Christ will be that of Satan and his demons.

> *Thou believest that there is one God; thou doest well: the devils also believe, and tremble. (James 2:19)*

There is a difference between believing and actual saving or victorious faith that runs a race with fortitude. The devils believe, but they will never be saved. Their belief is not faith that will save them. They will never fight the good fight of faith because their belief is a head knowledge and not a heart transformation.

Unless we have a heart transformation, God cannot lead our paths. Our life can only be led by God after we have experienced a life change that causes us to deny self daily. If we are to be guided by him, we need to trust him. We must not lean upon how we understand, see, or perceive something. There will be times the way, the direction, the course God says to take is going to seem contrary to what we think it should be.

It can seem utterly ridiculous to our natural man. Although there are many examples in the God's word of following God that could be contrary to our thoughts, I will give two positive examples of Abraham and Gideon and one negative example of the ten spies sent out to spy out the Promised Land.

Genesis 22:1–4 and Hebrews 11:17–19 disclose what an incredible fight of faith Abraham was faced with. He is told to offer Isaac who was his promised son and successor.

Now, he had to travel three days to where it was to take place. Can we even fathom the anguish, the anxiety, the turmoil Abraham's thinking was experiencing? How many of us would have traveled or continued the journey? How many of us would have given up the fight and left the race because of love for our loved one?

Joshua 24:15 says to choose. It is during the times we do not comprehend or it is the opposite of what we have done before that our choice to serve God is hard put to the test. We are so bent upon our own understanding that faith can be foreign to us. To walk by faith means to walk opposite of our thinking, our perception, our natural man.

We know Abraham's faith was recompensed and God supplied the offering, yet Abraham was truly walking on the water with only his faith keeping him afloat. How many of us would have sunk? How many of us truly have chosen to serve God no matter what? How many of us would stay in the race when what God asks goes against the very fiber of our being?

God promised Abraham in Genesis 22:18, *And in thy seed shall all the nations of the earth be blessed; because thou hast **obeyed** my voice.* He profited or was blessed because he chose to serve God and fight the good fight of faith and run his race with patience.

Our second positive example is found in Judges 7:1–7, 9–15 which reveals Gideon. Here we find the Midianites and the Amalekites were so numerous that they appeared to be like grasshoppers and their camels like the sand of the sea. Yet, God informs Gideon that he has too many men. After 22,000 leave and there are 10,000 remaining, God wants Gideon to go to battle with only 300 men.

What a choice it must have been for Gideon to allow God to lead him. He starts off with 32,000 men and God wants only 300 men. Was Gideon going to be led by God or lean upon his own understanding on warfare? Was Gideon going to call all the men back to fight? Was Gideon just going to walk away?

After all, common sense or logic says an army of 300 cannot beat tens of thousands. But God tells Gideon in verses Judges 7:9–15 to take his servant unto the outside of the armed men that were of the host. While there he hears a man relating his dream and its interpretation. The interpreter said, *this is nothing else save the sword of Gideon the son of Joash, a man of Israel: for into his hand hath God delivered Midian, and all the host.*

Gideon chose to serve God, fight the good fight of faith, run his race with persistence, and God gave the Israelites the victory. When we choose to follow God's lead, we profit in whatever He has led us into. Even if we do not see the profit in the natural, we know that all things work together for good to them who love God and are the called according to his purpose (Romans 8:28). If in God's will, all that happens in our life is working for our eternal profit. Unless we take our eyes off the present and focus upon eternity, we will not comprehend that everything in our life will be for our ultimate good.

Our negative example is found in Numbers 13:1–3; 17–33; 14:1–9, 22–38. We know up to this point, these had all witnessed the plagues of Egypt, the death of the firstborn, the parting of the Red Sea, God supplying the manna, etc. We saw when the Egyptians drowned in the Red Sea, the Israelites sang unto the Lord in Exodus 15, *he hath triumphed gloriously; the horse and his rider hath he thrown into the sea.*

After all this, the twelve spies came back from spying out the Promised Land for forty days. Keep in mind they were in the land for forty days without any harm or being detected.

> *27)And they told him, and said, We came unto the land whither thou sentest us, and surely it floweth with milk and honey; and this is the fruit of it. 28)Nevertheless the people be strong that dwell in the land, and the cities are walled, and very great: and moreover we saw the children of Anak there. 29)The Amalekites dwell in the land of the south: and the Hittites, and the Jebusites, and the Amorites, dwell in the mountains: and the Canaanites dwell by the sea, and by the coast of Jordan. 30)And Caleb stilled the people before Moses, and said, Let us go up at once, and possess it: for we are well able to overcome it. 31)But the men that went up with him said, We be not able to go up against the people; for they are stronger than we. 32) And they brought up an evil report of the land which they had searched unto the children of Israel, saying, The land, through which we have gone to search it, is a land that eateth up the inhabitants thereof; and all the people that we saw in it are men of a great stature. 33)And there we saw the giants, the sons of Anak, which come of the giants: and we were in our own sight as grasshoppers, and so we were in their sight. (Numbers 13:27-33)*

We see that Caleb tried to still the people and encourage them to trust God. They had chosen to serve God after crossing the Red Sea. But when the fight of good faith confronted them, they chose to quit. Instead of choosing to believe God who had told them He would deliver them out the hand of the Egyptians and bring them to a land flowing with milk and honey (Exodus 3:8), they chose to believe the lies of the evil report.

Their fears, their own understanding is what they leaned upon or trusted in and not God. It was God who parted the Red Sea and allowed them to walk on dry land while He drowned the Egyptians who endeavored to follow them.

God had delivered them out of the hands of the Egyptians and was fulfilling the rest of his promise to bring them into the land flowing with milk and honey. Yet, they chose to believe the evil report and not God.

Scripture makes clear they were unprofitable from that point on. They chose to forsake God and chose to believe lies. All who were twenty years and older died in the wilderness except Joshua and Caleb who went on to inherit the Promised Land. These two inherited because they fought the good fight of faith and ran their race with perseverance. The others chose not to fight the good fight of faith against their fleshly fears and chose to quit the race. Because of their choice not to believe and serve God, they lost what He had promised.

God puts battles before us to prove us, to prove the validity of our choice. Is our choice to be led by him genuine or is it surging because we witnessed the horse and rider drown in the sea? Will we choose to fight the giants or turn back because our logic or understanding says there is no way we can make it? Or will we choose to follow God's leading even when our flesh is in agony because it goes against what we feel, what we believe, what we have been taught, or what we think?

This book is to reveal what true faith in Jesus Christ can do. It is a faith that will fight the good fight of faith and overcome any battle the devil challenges us with. We cannot run our race and not expect sufferings, difficulties, adversities, struggles, griefs. However, if we sincerely choose God, we, as Abraham, Gideon, Joshua, and Caleb can be sure to be strengthened to fight the good fight of faith and run our race with patience until we finish!

Chapter 2

Press Forward

> *12)Not as though I had already attained, either were already perfect: but I follow after, if that I may apprehend that for which also I am apprehended of Christ Jesus. 13)Brethren, I count not myself to have apprehended: but this one thing I do, forgetting those things which are behind, and reaching forth unto those things which are before, 14)I press toward the mark for the prize of the high calling of God in Christ Jesus. (Philippians 3:12–14)*

THIS CHAPTER MAY NOT be a new truth, but it has not yet become a revelation or a reality in our understanding. Ofttimes as we hear a truth brought forth differently or from another perspective, it can trigger the light bulb of insight to transform our race.

Paul in the above verse is clearly stating he knows he has not apprehended or yet completed his race and received his final salvation. He has not yet fought the good fight of faith and run his race to the finish. He was in the process, but knew he had to forget what was behind and keep reaching forth unto what was waiting for him at the finish.

We know from 1 Corinthians 9:24–27 that Paul pictured himself and all Christians as athletes in a race. God's soldiers must comprehend that He wants us to keep striving, to keep on trying, to keep moving on, to never give up until we reach our goal. Our spiritual race is not dissimilar from a natural race. If we are running a race, we put forth all our strength and press forward with determination and tenacity in order to finish the course and receive the prize.

> 3)Thou therefore endure hardness, as a good soldier of Jesus Christ. 4)No man that warreth entangleth himself with the affairs of this life; that he may please him who hath chosen him to be a soldier. 5)And if a man also strive for masteries, yet is he not crowned, except he strive lawfully. (2 Timothy 2:3-5)

These verses were written to Timothy to encourage him to persevere. Such tenacity is not just for ministers, but all who have chosen to be soldiers in God's army. If we remain loyal to Christ and the gospel message, we will encounter and have to endure sufferings, hardship, adversity, grief, etc. We are in a war that lasts our entire life. We must fight the good fight of faith and run our race with patience until we take our last breath. It is not over until our death.

If we are going to finish our race, it is imperative to avoid all entanglements with the concerns of this life that could become a heavy weight and slow us down or take us off course. That is why we need to comprehend one weight will attract other weights like a magnet. It is like Marley in Dickens' Christmas Carol. He had been so concerned with the now of his life that he gave no thought for eternal life. In doing so, he was chained by those concerns.

I know what we choose to be concerned about here determines our eternal abode whether Heaven or Hell. However, Marley illustrates how the cares of this life can chain or bind us so we concentrate upon nothing else. When we do that, we are not fighting the good fight of faith nor are we running our race. We are continuously interweaving ourselves in the cares of this life until we are so wrapped up in the now that we forget about eternity.

Once we take our eyes off the race and focus upon this life and its struggles, we feel fear and worry about the whole shebang. Then we are full of anxiety and begin to doubt God is in control. This mentality continues in every area of our life until we are beset or defeated by unbelief. We no longer have our eyes upon fighting the good fight of faith or running the race set before us with perseverance. We are ensnared with this life and ignore eternity.

> *Wherefore seeing we also are compassed about with so great a cloud of witnesses, let us lay aside every weight, and the sin which doth so easily beset us, and let us run with patience the race that is set before us. (Hebrews 12:1)*

That is why in Philippians 3, Paul emphasizes the necessity of forgetting those things which are behind. We must forget any experience or sin that is in the past. It must be forgotten. We must lay it aside if we are to run the race set before us with patience.

We must not dwell upon past sufferings, fears, difficulties, failures, griefs, etc. Doing so will cause the weights to become heavier and heavier until all we are focused upon is the weight.

Imagine if Paul had dwelt upon what he did to believers before his conversion. He would have failed. Plus, we would have been the losers without his insight in the New Testament.

He says *forgetting*. That suggests that we are to ignore, drop, or lay aside those things that are behind. We no longer focus upon what is behind, but stay focused upon what is ahead.

Let me interject something here. The past is not just what happened before we were born again. The past is any weight or sin that has been confessed and repented of last year, month, yesterday, or as little as a second ago.

If we dwell, inhabit, abide, linger on whatever is past, it becomes a weight hindering us from going forwards. It keeps us in the past which means we are no longer fighting the good fight of faith nor are we running our race. Even wishing we had done something differently or wishing we had or had not done something. All regrets keep us in the past and prevent us from pressing forward.

It is important to always remember God does not bring up our past sins. When we repent, He forgives and forgets (Isaiah 43:25). If we are being reproached for our forgiven past, it is either our old nature, people, or fiery darts from the devil.

I always say that water over the dam is gone. It cannot be brought back up. Once we have asked God to forgive us, the sin is gone. It is over the dam. We must quit trying to reach for it or we will drown in the past.

We cannot reach forth unto those things which are before if we are looking behind. A racer looking behind will lose focus of what is ahead and lose the race. It is imperative that we forget or lay aside the past that could become a weight in hindering our pressing forward.

Such determination, such resoluteness, such tenacity, such willpower, such persistence, such single-mindedness is necessary to adhere to throughout our life. We must have tunnel vision when it comes to our race. Any distraction or temptation such as life's sufferings, worries, riches, evil desires, family, things, grief, etc. will become a weight or noose choking our commitment to Christ and preventing us from running our race.

Philippians 3:14 says, *I press toward the mark for the prize of the high calling of God in Christ Jesus.* The Apostle Paul knew the importance of pressing forward. How many of us comprehend the necessity of our doing likewise? Do we comprehend what pressing forward means? It is like rowing a boat against the current. It is strenuous, laborious, agonizing, but it is the only way to run our race.

There will be many times in which we will believe we cannot go on. Because of the arduous race, we will think we have had enough. However, that is the time we must deny self, fight our fleshly desire to quit, and bring ourselves into subjection to the will of God. We must force ourselves to go on. We must overpower or overrule the desire of our flesh and press forward.

We must never take our eyes off eternity and being with Jesus forever. When focused upon eternity, we forget the things that are behind, including the world (Egypt with its fleshly desires), and any sin that is past. It has no place in our present or our future life. When we come to Christ, old things pass away and all things become new; we are a new creature (2 Corinthians 5:17).

If we dwell or live in our past sins, failures, regrets, griefs, etc., we allow Satan to frustrate or overwhelm us with guilt.

> *There is therefore now no condemnation to them which are in Christ Jesus, who walk not after the flesh, but after the Spirit. (Romans 8:1)*

The word NOW in that verse is in the present tense. It means right now, at this present time, there is no condemnation (no judgment against, no sentence against, no guilt found). We are completely innocent because we are in a right relationship with Jesus Christ through faith in him.

We are being told that as we walk after the Spirit, we are free from condemnation (meaning guilt, eternal punishment). The reality or the present state of all who are in Christ and do not walk after the flesh (sin) but after the spirit are free from condemnation.

> *If we confess our sins, he is faithful and just to forgive us our sins, and to cleanse us from all unrighteousness. (1 John 1:9)*

We are those who are running our race in the Spirit and laying aside all weights. We are free from guilt and punishment because we have acknowledged our sin, we have owned up to our sin, we have come clean, and admitted our guilt. Because we have repented (no longer in that sin), we know He has forgiven us.

According to the Greek in the above scripture, forgive means to lay aside, put away, or remit. When Jesus forgives us, He remits our sin. He discharges us from it, He releases us from it. He pardons us. When we are pardoned, we receive clemency. The stain is wiped clean like it never happened.

Now, if Jesus has pardoned us because we are no longer living in sin, why do we allow guilt or shame to become a weight that keeps us down? Jesus laid it aside. That is why He wants us to lay aside any weight, including guilt.

Guilt is the sin of unbelief. It is calling God a liar. He says we are forgiven and our guilt is doubt or unbelief in him and his word. He has laid it aside. Now, we must do the same. We must comprehend there is **now**, through our repentance (our 180° turn), no condemnation or judgment against us. We have been pardoned. We must let it go, because God has already done so the moment we repented and asked for forgiveness. We need to comprehend our pardon has erased, irradicated our past. When we turn from our sin and are forgiven, our pardon is complete, irrevocable, and permanent.

With such a kingly pardon, let us rejoice in that freedom. Let us get rid of all those weights that have been weighing us down. Let us take our eyes off our forgiven sins, mistakes, regrets, and place them upon our race. Let us press forward, fight the good fight of faith, and run our race with steadfast persistence until we cross the finish line!

Chapter 3

Look Up For Help

1)I will lift up mine eyes unto the hills, from whence cometh my help. 2)My help cometh from the Lord, which made heaven and earth. 3) He will not suffer thy foot to be moved: he that keepeth thee will not slumber. 4)Behold, he that keepeth Israel shall neither slumber nor sleep. 5)The Lord is thy keeper: the Lord is thy shade upon thy right hand. 6)The sun shall not smite thee by day, nor the moon by night. 7)The Lord shall preserve thee from all evil: he shall preserve thy soul. 8)The Lord shall preserve thy going out and thy coming in from this time forth, and even for evermore. (Psalm 121:1-8)

IF WE ARE TO fight the good fight of faith and run the race set before us with patience, we must learn to look up to God for help. This life is full of suffering and man cannot be of help to us when we need supernatural assistance. He may offer natural help in the form of resources, advice, logic, condolence, etc., but it will not help us to overcome the spiritual battles of our life.

Look Up For Help

> *For we wrestle not against flesh and blood, but against principalities, against powers, against the rulers of the darkness of this world, against spiritual wickedness in high places. (Ephesians 6:12)*

Our fight is not physical, but spiritual. That truth must be paramount in our thinking if we are to conquer our daily struggles. We cannot fight evil adversaries in the natural. Because our fight of faith is supernatural, we must look up to God for help. He alone is our refuge, strength, and a very present help in times of trouble (Psalm 46:1).

If we look around, we would see the most perplexing, while being the most commonest feature of our human life, is suffering. Not one of us is spared from suffering. Anguish, distress, affliction, pain, heartache, grief, etc. come to all. We all share the different seasons of sorrow. We suffer a season of death, a season to weep, a season to mourn, a season to lose, etc. (Ecclesiastes 3)

Whatever differences there may be in mental endowments, wealth, or social position, there is among all of us, an unavoidable unity or oneness in suffering. None are free from suffering, whether king or peasant, whether employer or employee, whether adult or child. Suffering is a season that all mankind partakes of at various times.

Apparent and numerous as may be the physical suffering of mankind, there is a depth of mental distress of which those around do not know. We can all agree that a physical pain is easy to see. But sometimes there is a deep hurt that cannot be seen by the naked eye. Only God can reach into the depths of our heart and heal.

There are so many things that make our heart sorrowful. There are so many endeavors we do day and night with anxious thought and devoted labor, only to get nowhere. There are so many wounds inflicted by unjust and mean insinuations. There are so many words spoken with envy or heartless cruelty. Then there is the disappointments we feel by the faithlessness of someone we trusted.

> *5)Open rebuke is better than secret love. 6)Faithful are the wounds of a friend; but the kisses of an enemy are deceitful. (Proverbs 27:5-6)*

I am not speaking about the words of correction from someone who loves us and desires us to walk the walk that we talk. The Preacher revealed in Proverbs that type of correction is faithful, trustworthy, and loyal.

> *For whom the Lord loveth he chasteneth, and scourgeth every son whom he receiveth.* (Hebrews 12:6)

Hebrews reveals God corrects us because He loves us enough to show us our sin. It is tough love to tell the truth that may not be welcomed by the recipient. However, if God's soldiers want to serve God with a pure heart, correction would be accepted. We would desire him to reveal any error in our direction or judgment whether through the quickening of the Spirit or the faithful rebuke of a friend.

I had a circumstance as a young Christian where God required me to tell a friend about a situation. My insides were shuddering, but I knew it had to be done. Anyway, after I finished, the person looked at me and asked if I felt satisfied. I was stunned and responded that I did not find satisfaction in trying to restore him to a right relation with Christ. He was rude and said with friends like me who needs enemies.

It was several months later that he showed up at church again. He thanked me for being a true friend instead of an enemy who encouraged his sin. I will admit there have been other times that I was treated like an enemy and not someone who loved enough to tell the truth.

People's souls are in danger of Hell and too many Christians grease the pole for them instead of loving enough to pull them out of the devil's clutches with truth. Only truth will set people free from a sinful condition (John 8:32).

Psalms 21 causes us to think the Psalmist David had gone through something that produced suffering. Whatever his distress, he was influenced to write this song of praise and honor to God for his help in time of trouble. David knew the Lord was the keeper of his people who trust and rely on him. God's children are constantly under his shield, defense, and attentive care. He will never leave nor forsake us (Hebrews 13:5). It is our unbelief that causes us to believe we are alone when going through suffering.

David was aware of God's abiding presence and made clear that during our sufferings, we must look up to him for help. He knew his only help during any suffering comes from God. Whatever it was he suffered, he learned to look up to God for his support. He did not seek earthly assistance. How do I believe that? He said, *I will lift up mine eyes unto the hills*.

David claimed to look up to the hills. Hills do not mean that he looked up to some mountain, per say, as if his help was from any mountain or physical structure. David knew no mountain could help him. He looked to God for his help. When he looked up, it was upon the mountain heights of Judea that stood on Mt. Zion.

On those hills, the temple stood, the pride of the Hebrew. It was there that Jehovah localized his presence. Mt. Zion was where the people had uplifting intimacy with their God. The heartfelt and dearest memories of life huddled around the experiences of the sanctuary. It was there the sad heart lost its burden. It was there that God gave a peace that enabled the most sorrowful heart to be uplifted.

David had decided to look onto Jehovah, who dwelleth on Mt. Zion, or rather, in the highest heavens. When we truly love God, we realize our only times of comfort in sufferings, has come from him. He alone is our peace (Ephesians 2:14). He alone gives rest to the weary soul (Matthew 11:28). He alone meets our every need (Philippians 4:19). He alone delivers us from the snare of the fowler (Psalms 91:3). He alone preserves us from all evil (Psalm 121:7).

> And he said unto me, My grace is sufficient for thee: for my strength is made perfect in weakness. Most gladly therefore will I rather glory in my infirmities, that the power of Christ may rest upon me. (2 Corinthians 12:9)

In order for us to walk in the revelation David had of Jehovah, we must comprehend God's grace. Let me give the example the Lord gave me some years ago of his grace. I was thinking about the storm at sea in Mark 4, and contemplating the different reactions between the disciples and Jesus.

The disciples were frantic as the boat filled up with water, whereas Jesus was in the hinder part of the ship, asleep on a pillow. I asked the Lord what is that story teaching besides that you could calm the raging storm? I sense a deeper meaning as to why you could sleep. I know you trusted Father to get you to the other side, but how could you be so calm and sleep in the middle of a raging storm?

He told me God's grace was sufficient, for his strength was made perfect in any human weakness. He then showed me a hurricane and the eye of the storm. It was quite a revelation, for I saw the eye represented his grace. Yes, the storm was still intense all around, but there was an incredible peace in the eye. The eye was calm and peaceful.

However, if we touched the eyewall, it was dangerous. The winds of the eyewall are the scariest, nastiest, gnarliest part of the storm. They form an unbroken line of extremely powerful downpours where the winds can roar at 140 miles per hour. What that is teaching is that if we step outside of his grace (the eye), we will find ourselves in a cataclysm by the storm.

Jesus is teaching us that as we rest in his grace (in the eye), we are asleep with him. If we allow fear to overwhelm us, we are outside his grace (at the eyewall) with the disciples. How many times have we found ourselves at the eyewall because of not looking to God but leaning to our own understanding? Too many times we allow ourselves to keep our eyes on the storm (trial, grief, etc.) and not trusting his grace that is sufficient for any suffering.

Whereas if we yield to his grace, that is sufficient, we will have the peace that passeth all understanding no matter how furious things may be around us. His grace gives us the strength to rest in him through all storms, obstacles, grief, sufferings, etc. It reveals that nothing can interfere with our fighting the good fight of faith or running the race set before us with patience or perseverance as long as we stay in his grace (the eye of the storm).

The only time there is interference or obstruction is when we succumb to the frenzy of the storm instead of yielding to his grace that will keep us composed and tranquil. In other words, we step out of the eye of the storm into the eyewall.

Back to the suffering brought on by hurtful, hateful, and unjust words. Perhaps the Psalmist was feeling like the Apostle Paul who had been forsaken by all men as recorded in 2 Timothy 4:16. Paul too, had learned that when all others forsake us, turn against us, that the Lord will never leave nor forsake us (Hebrews 13:5).

> *In my distress I called upon the Lord, and cried unto my God: he heard my voice out of his temple, and my cry came before him, even into his ears. (Psalms 18:6)*
>
> *I sought the Lord, and he heard me, and delivered me from all my fears. (Psalm 34:4)*

The advantage God's people have is knowing the truths that God hears our cries of distress and delivers us. Those who do not know him have no consolation in their suffering. They have no supernatural help to sustain them and have no peace that passes all understanding. Seeking earthly help will not give the grace necessary to overcome the darkness trying to engulf.

However, the children of God are assured of his help whenever we call upon him for assistance. As we yield to his grace, we look up to him for the strength necessary to overcome whatever comes our way.

No, the storm may not cease, the turmoil may still continue, the grief may still be there. But in his grace (the eye of the storm), we will find the peace necessary to continue our fight of faith and run our race. As we look up to God for help, his grace, his strength, his power enables our weakness to do what we cannot do in the natural. As we yield to his grace, we are empowered to do what seems impossible to man (Luke 1:37).

This truth is quite clear in our salvation experience. We had no power in ourselves to save us. However, God's grace gave us the supernatural power to believe (have faith) in his word to save. When we believed, God replaced our weakness for his strength that translated us from spiritual death to spiritual life (Ephesians 2:8).

For a better understanding about the miracle that took place at our spiritual birth, see the first chapter in my book, *Faith's Journey Confronts Obstacles: Instructing God's Soldiers to Overcome in His Armor*. Once we comprehend God's grace allows his strength to be made perfect in our weakness, we understand his grace is all sufficient for whatever we need.

It is time for God's people to perceive, as David, there is no help in anyone or anything outside of God. Our help comes from him who made heaven and earth. We must expect help from no other source but him. David believed God is; therefore, he believed God is a rewarder of them that diligently seek him (Hebrews 11:6).

What is David teaching us in Psalm 121? He is teaching us to pillar or foundation ourselves upon God as a God all-sufficient for us. We must not rely upon men, resources, instruments, etc., nor make flesh our arm (Jeremiah 17:5).

We are NOT to put our trust, our all, in anything or anyone, but God. He, alone, will never let us down. God will never disappoint us and give faithlessness to our faith in him. God will never inflict with some malicious gain on his part. God is completely without any selfish means in anything and everything He does. His desire is for us to spend eternity with him. Whatever we must overcome and endure here is for us to be strengthened in the faith that enables us to ignore the storm, gets in the eye or rests in his grace, and presses forward to the finish line.

Yes, we may look to others for help on the natural scale. God gave gifts for such offices or responsibilities. We are told not to close our bowels of compassion to those in need (1 John 3:17). God uses people to meet the needs of the brethren. Also, ministers are called to perfect or to help mature the sheep in the faith.

In this chapter, we are speaking about the help that no man, woman, child, etc. can give. It is when all our natural is exhausted or when our natural is weakening, and to go on, we need supernatural help from his grace. Only his strength will get us through whatever we are facing or enduring.

Look Up For Help

It is those times when we are tempted to weaken, those times that we feel like we are becoming weary in well-doing, those times when all seems to be against us, those times where we want to stop fighting the good fight of faith, and quit the race. It is those times, when, if it was not for God's grace that gives us supernatural strength, we could not go on.

We will lift up our eyes. Why do we lift up our eyes? Is it because we depend upon the powers of the earth, upon men, upon the natural, upon the arm of flesh? NO, our confidence is in God and God alone. We must look beyond the natural realm of help, and look up to God.

God is informing us to realize all our HELP is laid upon him, in his love, in his power, and in his goodness. We must bring help from God, by faith in his promises. What I am clarifying is that God, through his faith, brought all things into existence. Our faith, in him and his ability, brings his promises into existence.

God received what He believed; we receive what we believe. Do we believe He can make what seems impossible to be possible (Luke 1:37)? Do we believe He can do exceeding abundantly above all that we ask or think according to the power (of faith) that worketh in us (Ephesians 3:20)?

David knew God was a person of his word. When he called on God for help, he expected just that. He expected, by faith, that God would help him. He knew it is only God that can help when there is nothing left but the desire to retreat, to escape, to withdraw. When we want to stop fighting and want to quit the race, God is there, through his grace, to provide whatever supernatural help we require to continue.

> 38)For I am persuaded, that neither death, nor life, nor angels, nor principalities, nor powers, nor things present, nor things to come, 39)Nor height, nor depth, nor any other creature, shall be able to separate us from the love of God, which is in Christ Jesus our Lord. (Romans 8:38-39)

If we are going to learn to look up to God, it is imperative to believe God's love for us is so great that nothing can separate us from it. He promises to be with us always, even unto the end of the world (Matthew 28:20). We are never in any dark time of storm alone. It is not what we feel that is our strength, but what we know. Whether we sense his presence or not, faith knows He is always with us. God's soldiers walk by faith and not by sight or feelings (2 Corinthians 5:7).

> *Thy word is a lamp unto my feet, and a light unto my path. (Psalms 119:105)*

When we comprehend God's love, we realize his word is our light to guide us through the darkest storms. We know we cannot walk outside at night without a light. There could be various situations to trip us, unseen holes to cause us to stumble, unknown predators to attack us, etc. As God's soldiers, we are constantly walking through a shroud of evil bent on destroying us.

Without a knowledge of God's love and his word, we have no light or way to overcome the darkness trying to engulf us. As we walk through a dark and evil world, God's word will help us evade the traps that have been set by the enemy to ambush us. Although we may not see light literally, with an understanding of God's ever-presence and endless love, we believe his word. Without the light of his word to lighten our path through the dark storms, we will fall.

What do I mean that his word is our light to get us through the dark storms? He promises that we can do all things through Christ which strengthens us (Philippians 4:13). It does not matter how black the storm, how weak we may feel, or how strong our adversary appears. God promises that his grace is sufficient to give us his supernatural strength to endure, confront, or overcome whatever storm comes our way.

We know we can do all things through Christ. We know He loves us, for that was proven on Calvary (John 3:16). We know He is always with us (Hebrews 13:5; Matthew 28:20). Thus, we look up to God, trust his grace to give us the strength to keep fighting the good fight of faith and run the race set before us with perseverance until we finish!

Chapter 4

Other Gods

Thou shalt have none other gods before me.
(Deuteronomy 5:7)

2)And the word of the Lord came unto me, saying, 3)Son of man, these men have set up their idols in their heart, and put the stumblingblock of their iniquity before their face: should I be enquired of at all by them? 4)Therefore speak unto them, and say unto them, Thus saith the Lord God; Every man of the house of Israel that setteth up his idols in his heart, and putteth the stumblingblock of his iniquity before his face, and cometh to the prophet; I the Lord will answer him that cometh according to the multitude of his idols. 5)That I may take the house of Israel in their own heart, because they are all estranged from me through their idols. 6)Therefore say unto the house of Israel, Thus saith the Lord God; Repent, and turn yourselves from your idols; and turn away your faces from all your abominations. (Ezekiel 14:2–6)

WHAT DOES GOD MEAN by commanding us to have no other gods before him? We find the answer in Ezekiel. All idols are false gods that we worship above the Lord who delivered us from the bondage of sin.

Other gods are idols that we put before God in our heart. It is what becomes our center of worship. It could be a job, a person, an activity, a thing, a loss, a grief, or even self. Whatever we meditate upon more than God, whatever drives our thoughts and actions, becomes our god. Other gods that draw our affection away from God dull our spiritual hearing and harden our hearts to the things of God. Any idol will challenge the sovereignty, the power, the authority of God.

The scriptures in Ezekiel chapter fourteen inform us that any idol or other god we set up in our heart will become a self-induced stumblingblock. An idol cannot be set up unless we allow it as a desire in our heart. We choose of our own free-will to erect that other god. Perceive fully, if not removed, it will cause us to stumble in the faith. Thereby obstructing our fighting the good fight of faith and running the race set before us.

> *But be ye doers of the word, and not hearers only, deceiving your own selves. (James 1:22)*

Whenever we become a hearer only of God's word and do not adhere to obeying it, we have opened the door for other gods to be set up in our heart. How is that? Because our other god or idol starts with self who does not believe it must do what the Scriptures say. We cannot blame anyone if we become deceived. We heard the word, decided not to obey, and became deceived by our own selves. We choose to deny the scripture has reference to our life and is not important for us to obey. We have chosen to disregard the importance of having no other gods before the Lord. All idols will cause us to ignore fighting the good fight of faith and running the race set before us.

That is why the Lord is resolute for us to have none other gods before him. God will not permit any rival with him. We are to worship him and only him. He knows if we serve other gods, we will not persevere to overcome this life. If we do not persevere, there will be no crossing the finish line.

And thou shalt love the Lord thy God with all thy heart, and with all thy soul, and with all thy mind, and with all thy strength: this is the first commandment. (Mark 12:30)

No person, place, thing, etc. is to have preeminence in our heart that could interfere with our loving the Lord exclusively. He must take precedence over anyone and everything in our life. This is not cruelty on God's part. He knows if we are not totally dedicated to him, we will position other gods first. If we position another god before him, He is not our God.

It is essential for us to understand the importance of loving God above all else. As we love God with all our **heart**, there is naught that can compare to our devotion to him. We are willing to give up all for him in order to please and glorify him in all things. God becomes our greatest desire, the center of all our affections, our whole life becomes his to direct. If God is not first in our life, we will set up an idol or other god (person, place, thing) that will take priority over him. How else do we think sin takes hold? It is when other gods (sin) in our heart takes preeminence over God.

When we love God with all our **soul**, it means with our very breath. This love causes us to love God more than our life. The martyrs mentioned in my book, *Satan's Strategy to Torment Through Physical Ambush* definitely loved God more than their own life. If they had not, they could not have suffered such persecution for the name of Christ. In my first book, *Storms Are Faith's Workout*, I explained self-love. When self is first, we will never fight the good fight of faith that is willing to give our life for Christ.

To love God with all our **mind** is to love him with all our intellectual power or our understanding. Our mind is where we conceive, judge, or reason. It yields our intentions, our principles, and our plans. Everything entering our mind must be conceived, evaluated, and analyzed. How it is analyzed determines our actions and our beliefs. Whatever we do is the result of what has been through our thought process. Our mind is the center of our will, and our will is where we choose to believe God or to not believe him. It is where we choose to obey God or not to obey him. It is where God is God or other gods are god. It is where we choose to fight or not to fight. It is where we choose to run or to quit the race.

Loving God with all our **strength** means we are willing to persevere in our faith walk when battles are challenging and we are physically exhausted from running our arduous race. We place all our efforts and energies into pleasing God and doing his will. It can require us to deny self to make tough decisions and choices that will agonize our flesh. In short, we will with resolute persistence fight the good fight of faith as Jesus did when going to Calvary no matter how severe the pain of our choice may be upon our flesh.

> *Wherefore seeing we also are compassed about with so great a cloud of witness, let us lay aside every weight, and the sin which doth so easily beset us, and let us run with patience the race that is set before us.(Hebrews 12:1)*

The weights are hindrances or stumblingblocks obstructing the progress of our race. Whatever we desire in our flesh often erect other gods in our heart. That idol will become a stumblingblock hindering us from fighting the good fight of faith.

Is it the desire for a better job? Is it the desire for a husband or a wife? Is it the desire to have children? Is it the desire for a better house? All of these desires may be a promise from the Lord taking too long for fruition. Our flesh has convinced us perhaps He meant for it to be this way, etc.

Seriously, how many of us have been given a promise, became weary in the wait or well-doing, and decided how the promise will be accomplished. We start to rationalize what God must have meant until our logic has overruled faith. It is no longer running our race with perseverance that believes God can do the impossible (Luke 1:37), but how can we cause the promise to materialize.

> *1)Now Sarai Abram's wife bare him no children: and she had an handmaid, an Egyptian, whose name was Hagar. 2)And Sarai said unto Abram, Behold now, the Lord hath restrained me from bearing: I pray thee, go in unto my*

Other Gods

maid; it may be that I may obtain children by her. And Abram hearkened to the voice of Sarai. (Genesis 16:1–2)

This story is an excellent example of how idols or other gods in the heart can become a stumblingblock where we stop fighting the good fight of faith and decide how to make the promise happen. Abraham and Sarah desperately wanted a child. When God gives us a promise, we can become weary in waiting for it to come to pass (Galatians 6:9). That is a dangerous place for us to be. God never puts a time frame from the seed of the promise until it is harvested. Galatians 6:9 makes obvious we can become fatigued in our waiting or our well-doing. During the time of the wait, we can start to lean on our own understanding.

Sarah believed there was no way for her to give birth at her age and decided to help God out. Abraham knew God had promised him an heir who would come forth out of his own bowels, and he knew Sarah was beyond child-bearing age. So he agrees with Sarah that Hagar must be the way for it to be accomplished. Their desire for the heir was the other god in their heart that became the stumblingblock which caused them to lean upon their own understanding and take things into their own hands.

Of course, that other god is a stumblingblock threatening Israel and the whole world today with Ishmael (Islam). As Ishmael hated Isaac, the child of faith, Muslims hate Isaac's progeny (Jews and Christians) today. The fact is as Ishmael was the child of the flesh, whatever we bring forth in the flesh will have negative consequences.

Let us understand how other gods or idols become stumblingblocks and can be set up in our heart through preachers teaching wrong doctrines. For instance, they preach the gospel of prosperity where many have stumbled seeking after riches instead of seeking the Kingdom of God first and his righteousness. They preach a doctrine of carnality that teaches once saved, we can indulge in sin because Jesus took our punishment for sin. We are now free to live as we please. If we do not get rid of the other god of self-indulgence, we will not fight the fight of faith nor run the race set before us that requires self-denial.

How many have become so deceived into believing once we accept Jesus as Savior we can live however we want. There is no difference in our life than those of the world. We have become hearers only of the word and not doers. The deception causes us to live in sin. When God's word says if we do it, we will not inherit the Kingdom of God, He means it. God is not a respecter of persons. Sin will be judged as sin if not repented of even if we believe we are God's child (Romans 2:11–13). Sin is anything contrary to what God considers holiness, godliness, righteousness, etc. We are so deceived through being a hearer only that we shrug it off as the loss of some reward.

I have some laugh and say we may lose a crown or a reward, but at least we will be there. It must grieve the Lord who has made clear that we inherit all things and He will be our God ONLY if we overcome (Revelation 21:7). If we do not repent, do a 180° turn, it is not a reward that will be lost, but Heaven that will be missed. Some have used 1 Corinthians 6:11 and claimed because we are washed, sanctified, and justified, we are no longer sinners.

That Scripture denotes because we have repented (turned from our sin), we have been justified by the Holy Spirit. It signifies we are no longer guilty. We cannot remain *in* the sin and believe we are no longer guilty of such sin. Any sin in our life is an idol or other god. We must repent, turn from our idols, and turn our face from our abominations. All other gods are abominations to the Lord.

A sinner's prayer does not guarantee anything. Scripture is clear that if we turn from righteousness and indulge in unrighteousness without repentance, all our righteousness will be forgotten and we will die in that sin (Ezekiel 18:24).

To believe otherwise is deception and is utterly absurd. What we have done is set up sin as an idol or other god in our heart and allowed it to become a stumblingblock. That is how deceived many are and have believed the lies of the devil over the truth of God's word. When we accept the evil report, we lose God's promise. We have become comfortable walking the wide and broad path and have no intention of fighting the good fight of faith nor running the race set before us that requires self-denial.

Only as we love God more than our life and become aware of the necessity to contend (struggle against difficulties or opposition) will we recognize other gods that could be set up in our heart. As we allow the Holy Spirit to identify a potential stumblingblock, we will fight the good fight of faith and run our race with steadfast endurance until the end!

Chapter 5

Spiritual Authority

Behold, I give unto you power to tread on serpents and scorpions, and over all the power of the enemy: and nothing shall by any means hurt you. (Luke 10:19)

THIS CHAPTER WILL ADMONISH us to comprehend in order for us to fight the good fight of faith and run the race set before us, we must walk in spiritual authority over Satan. If we do not take the authority Christ has given us, the devil will take what is not his to take. He has been conquered by Christ who has given his disciples (we who are born again) authority over all the power of the devil.

It is imperative for us to grasp hold of that truth. The devil has no power or authority over the child of God. If he gets the better of us, it is because we have forfeited our power and submitted to his. This is a sad reality in the lives of many claiming to be born again. We are walking in surrender to Satan instead of walking in the authority over him that Christ gave us.

SPIRITUAL AUTHORITY

> *13) Then certain of the vagabond Jews, exorcists, took upon them to call over them which had evils spirits the name of the Lord Jesus, saying, We adjure you by Jesus whom Paul preacheth. 14) And there were seven sons of one Sceva, a Jew, and chief of the priests, which did so. 15) And the evil spirit answered, and said, Jesus I know, and Paul I know; but who are ye? 16) And the man in whom the evil spirit was leaped on them, and overcame them, and prevailed against them, so that they fled out of that house naked and wounded. (Acts 19:13–16)*

Many of God's soldiers are receiving similar reactions as those of the sons of Sceva. It is not because we are not Christ's as they were not. It is because we are ignorant or unaware of our authority over the enemy. Ignorance of our God-given power, causes us to be unknowing or heedless of Satan's strategies. We tend to walk in our own understanding or what we think is best for our life with little or no comprehension of God's word. Without knowing what Christ has given to us, we will not walk as victors but as vanquished.

> *Lest Satan should get an advantage of us: for we ae not ignorant of his devices. (2 Corinthians 2:11)*

This Scripture has a two-fold meaning which is imperative for us to comprehend. Firstly, because we are **not** ignorant of Satan's devices, he will not get the advantage over us. The second meaning is that if we **are** ignorant of Satan's devices, he will get the advantage over of us.

When the devil gets the advantage over a Christian, he or she (the Christian) comes out of the encounter like the sons of Sceva. We flee like cowards or the conquered. Our flesh takes control and we become disheartened, discouraged, and spiritually weakened.

The troubling part is that when this happens or when difficulty or calamity hit, we blame God. But the blunder is really ours. It is not God's fault when we claim to be his child and are ignorant of Satan's devices, his cunning, his trickery, or his methods. It is not God's fault that we are unaware of the fact that we have power or authority over the devil. It is not God's fault when we insist on being a hearer only and not a doer of his word.

> *My people are destroyed for lack of knowledge: because thou hast rejected knowledge, I will also reject thee. (Hosea 4:6)*

Hosea reveals the law of reciprocity. In other words, it is the result of what happens when something is done. Let me give an example of reciprocity. We work and the employer gives us our wages. When God says if we do something, He will do this or that, He reciprocates or gives in return. According to Hosea, God is saying that if we, of our own free-will, reject his knowledge, his laws, or his principles, we will pay the consequences of that choice. It is his law of reciprocity being carried out.

That is why we can find ourselves like the sons of Sceva after a spiritual encounter with the devil. If we do not take the spiritual authority given to us, Satan will defeat us. Ignorance will leave us with the consequences of that lack of knowledge. God promised if we choose to be ignorant, there is reciprocity.

> *Study to shew thyself approved unto God, a workman that needeth not to be ashamed, rightly dividing the word of truth. (2 Timothy 2:15)*

For any of us today, who claim to be a Christian, to lack knowledge or to be ignorant of Satan's devices is intentional. That may seem harsh, but it is truth. We have access to much media of the word of God. There is not only the written word, but it is available on CD's, etc.

There is no excuse for us to be ignorant. If we are, we have intentionally chosen to reject the knowledge that would keep us from being destroyed. If we study his word, we will have the knowledge necessary to fight the good of faith and to run with perseverance the race set before us.

I do not know how many times I have heard Christians claim there is no time to read the Bible because of our work schedule, our classes, etc. Yet, how many have time to play games, watch television, go out to eat, or whatever? Because of this, Satan and his demons are getting the advantage over us. Christians, who are not to be ignorant of Satan's devices, seem to be as ignorant of the things of God and the tactics of Satan as were the sons of Sceva who did not know the Lord.

> *Let this mind be in you which was also in Christ Jesus. (Philippians 2:5)*

Think of that. Was Jesus ignorant of Satan's devices, cunning, methods, or stratagems? Of course not. He knew the modus operandi of Satan. Because He was aware of Satan's devices, Christ knew how the enemy works. Because Jesus knew his enemy, He knew how to combat or to overcome all the tactics or motives of the forces of evil. Nothing hindered Christ from fighting the good fight of faith or running the race set before him with persistence. He was not hindered from finishing his course that ended at Calvary.

As Christ recognized and knew the enemy, Satan and the demons knew Christ. Let us understand something here. Satan and his demons, the fallen angels who follow him, are personal intelligences.

The devil is a real spirit personality and so are his demons. What does the word personality mean? The simplest definition is the power of thinking, the power of feeling, and the power of willing. It is time for us to realize that Satan has intelligence that is keener, sharper, and craftier than our intelligence. That means the intelligence of Satan and his demons, who are also spirit personalities, is more acute than the intellect we possess. They are spiritual, supernatural beings and we are physical, natural beings. Flesh and blood cannot conquer or wrestle against spiritual wickedness (Ephesians 6:12).

No matter how smart or how intellectual we may be, we will never outsmart or out maneuver the forces of Satan in the natural. Yet, God's soldiers insist upon being led by carnal or worldly ways. We use our own understanding or whatever else is from the flesh or sensual. Then when forced to face Satan, we find ourselves running away like the sons of Sceva.

Listen to me, if we are to be wiser than Satan and his hosts, it must be through the Spirit. As the devil is a spirit personality, so is the Holy Spirit. But the Holy Spirit is the Creator of the other spirits. Remembering that Satan and his demons were created by God Almighty will give us the advantage when attacked by the enemy. As we yield to the Holy Spirit, we are enabled supernaturally to **stand** in the full armor of God against any assaults Satan may throw at us (Ephesians 6:13).

> *For though we walk in the flesh, we do not war after the flesh: For the weapons of our warfare are not carnal, but mighty through God to the pulling down of strong holds. (2 Corinthians 10:3-4)*

We have to know the devil is not only smarter (has far superior intelligence over us), but he is spirit. We are flesh and blood and we cannot battle with spirit beings. Yes, we live or walk in the natural or fleshly because we are flesh and blood. However, as many Christians have found out, the hard way, we cannot war after the natural. The weapons that we are to use must be God's. Why is that so? Because God is the Creator of wisdom, intelligence, He cannot be outwitted by his creation. Any weapons the devil may use are inferior to God's weapons. The devil has no power over his Creator.

Think of that truth. If we create something in the physical, can what we create take power over us? It may be used for evil, but the thing itself cannot take authority over its creator. We know how we created it and know how to destroy it.

Only God, who is Satan's Creator, knows how to overcome him. Only God is Omniscient or all knowing; He is the Creator of knowledge. If Satan and his diabolical crew can get us in the flesh, we are beaten before we start. That is why we must learn to put on the whole armor of God and stand in his supernatural power when facing the devil and his demons. To comprehend God's full armor, I suggest reading my book, *Faith's Journey Confronts Obstacles: Instructing God's Soldiers to Overcome in His Armor*.

If we try to take on the devil in our flesh, it is like using a water gun to defeat him. That sounds ridiculous, but that is exactly what we look like to Satan and the demons in our flesh. Simply put, we are defeated before we start.

Spiritual Authority

> *The thief cometh not, but for to steal, and to kill, and to destroy: I am come that they might have life, and that they might have it more abundantly. (John 10:10)*

Satan comes to bring death (spiritual death). Christ comes to bring life (spiritual life). Think of that. Now, let us look at our Christian life. Are we more spiritual than carnal? Do we spend most of our time in the flesh or in the spirit? Do we complain, bicker, call people names, etc. or do we deny self? Do we discuss spiritual things or things of little value when compared to the spiritual things of God? If we are more carnal than spiritual, we are submitting to Satan who is keeping us carnally influenced. He is setting us up to destroy us. We will end up like the sons of Sceva.

> *And be not conformed to this world: but be ye transformed by the renewing of your mind, that ye may prove what is that good, and acceptable, and perfect, will of God. (Romans 12:2)*

God's soldiers must be transformed from the likeness of this world into the likeness of Christ. This is only accomplished by the renewing, the renovating, the refurbishing, the repairing of our minds (Romans 12:2). As long as we continue to partake of this world and its way, our mind will never be renewed. The only way for our mind to be transformed from fleshly minded to spiritually minded is changing the media it is programmed with.

Too many Christians are not reading, studying, and meditating upon the word of God, which is the only way to receive the mind of Christ. This means the thinking, the discerning, the reasoning, etc. of Christ. When we walk in the mind of Christ, we no longer walk in our natural mind and its carnality. Walking in the mind of Christ enables us to fight the good fight of faith and run the race set before us with unwavering tenacity.

> *Be sober, be vigilant; because your adversary the devil, as a roaring lion, walketh about, seeking whom he may devour: whom resist steadfast in the faith. (1 Peter 5:8-9a)*

This is a hard truth, but many in the Church are not sober. We are intoxicated with the things of the flesh and the love of the world.

We are not vigilant. Many of us are so ignorant of Satan's desire and tactics for our destruction, that we march right alongside of him. By the time, many of us realize who we are yielding to, it is too late. For we have been overcome or overpowered as the sons of Sceva.

Satan and his demons never slithered up on Jesus, Paul, etc. They were watching for him. Their heart was tuned into God, their eyes were anointed with spiritual eye salve, and they recognized the devices of Satan. Because they possessed eyes to see and ears to hear, they were blessed in their ability to identify the strategies of the devil (Matthew 13:16).

God knows every move the devil is making, and He knows the moves he will make before he makes them. That is why those with the mind of Christ who walk in Spirit and in truth are not taken off guard by the enemy. Do not get me wrong, the devil will still come as he did with Christ. However, if we walk in the spiritual authority we have over him, he will not win over us.

> *Behold I give unto you power to tread on serpents and scorpions, and over all the power of the enemy: and nothing shall by any means hurt you. (Luke 10:19)*

Okay, why are the serpents and scorpions stealing, killing, and destroying the lives of so many of us professing to belong to Christ? It is quite simple. Just because we have the spiritual authority does not mean we walk in it.

This authority or power is not a carnal, fleshly, or natural authority, it is a spiritual or supernatural authority. It is letting Christ's mind think in us. In fact, it is being crucified with Christ and living by his faith or Godlike faith (Galatians 2:20). To comprehend Godlike faith, see my book, *Satan Has No Authority Over God's Soldier: Illuminating Godlike Faith*. An understanding of God's faith will revolutionize our faith walk.

It is us standing in the natural realm that we see, but it is having no fleshly part in the standing. We yield ourselves to Christ, clothe ourselves in God's full armor, and then our spirit being is one with his. It is then Jesus standing in the spirit world. In other words, the devil sees us, but he also sees him who is in us.

As we submit ourselves to God, resist Satan, he will flee from us (James 4:7). Listen to me, Satan is no match for Jesus Christ who is his Creator. He is well aware that Jesus will destroy him in the end (Matthew 8:29). It is us who must grasp the truth that Satan has no power or authority over us who walk in Spirit and in truth.

Yet, how many of us constantly walk in the flesh or carnality? God wants us to get out of ourselves, our selfish pleasures, and stand against the devil as his soldiers wholly armed in his full armor. He has done all to give us the spiritual authority over Satan. Now, He expects us to take that authority, walk in it, and be victorious.

We must quit trying to fight a spirit with supernatural powers with our natural or fleshly weapons. Satan knows if he can keep us in the flesh, he can keep us defeated. God's soldiers must stop playing tiddly winks with the devil and letting him win. We must stop being on the defensive, passive and take the offensive, aggressive stance with the devil.

God's disciples have spiritual authority over the devil. Instead of allowing him to push us back, we must press forward and take ground from him. Chapter twelve will help us comprehend aggressive warfare.

We should know the difference between our being in the flesh and in the Spirit. Galatians 5:19–21 name the works of the flesh. Perhaps we are not adulterers, fornicators, etc. However, do we hate, do we envy (jealous, greed, resentment, covet, begrudge), do we look to strive (brawl, fight, battle, compete)? We need to stop yielding to our flesh and start yielding to God. We must put our flesh and its lust (desire, yearn, crave) under and bring our body into subjection to Christ. We must stop being the victim when we are the victor.

God's soldiers need to remember that it was through his faith that God created all things. His faith is capable of doing the impossible. There is nothing that God cannot do (Matthew 19:26). When we became born again and filled with the Holy Spirit of God, He gave us all a measure of faith that is capable of doing the impossible through Him (Luke 17:6). We are not the ones doing the impossible, but God through us. Godlike faith arises in us and enables God to be God and do what is impossible to man (Mark 10:27).

It is essential to know that we know we have spiritual authority over Satan and that he has no authority over us. As we walk in the mind of Christ, we walk in the power that gives no place to the devil, his demons, or his diabolical plans to destroy us. We are aware of Satan, his designs, his tactics, his obstacles, his strategies, his devices, etc., and they are prohibited from prospering. God's soldiers stand in his full armor, fight the good fight of faith, and run the race set before us with staunch fortitude until we cross the finish line!

Chapter 6

Apathetic Indifference

28)And now, little children, abide in him; that, when he shall appear, we may have confidence, and not be ashamed before him at his coming. 29)If ye know that he is righteous, ye know that every one that doeth righteousness is born of him. (1 John 2:28-29)

Your throne, O God, is forever and ever, a sceptre of righteousness is the sceptre of thy kingdom.
(Hebrews 1:8)

THE LORD HAS REVEALED there is an apathetic indifference or inactive zeal for fighting the good fight of faith and running the race in many claiming to be Christians. Many have become complacent and sit in the pew of do-nothing. We go to church and sit there in a state of fake righteousness, when, in fact, our lives outside of church reflect unrighteousness.

It is not what we pretend to be in church, but what we exhibit at home, work, etc. that reveals who we really are. What do we talk about? How do we treat others? What do we meditate upon? What do we listen to? What do we watch or read? Are we meditating on God's word or the words of false ministers? Are we listening to those teaching an ear tickling message? Are we watching, reading, and believing what these false ministers say? Have we quit fighting the good fight of faith? Have we walked away from the race?

> *Be not deceived: evil communications corrupt good manners. (1 Corinthians 15:33)*

It is a sad truth, but many are deceiving themselves. We cannot take in corruption and not have corruption come out. We cannot fellowship with bad company or evil associations and it not corrupt our morals and our character. If we believe we can sow something and not reap what has been sown, we are deceived (Galatians 6:7). If we believe evil communications will not corrupt our life, we are deceived.

Are we showing forth the praises of him who called us out of darkness and translated us into his marvelous light? (1 Peter 2:9). How many times do we leave church and go forth to gossip, indulge in sin, and grieve the Holy Spirit?

It is a distressing truth, but many of God's soldiers are alienating themselves from God because of hypocritical lives. We no longer have an enthusiastic passion to run the race set before us with dedication, but an apathetic indifference that no longer fights the good fight of faith.

We are no longer zealous for the things of God, but the things of this world. We are no longer concerned about righteous living. God is no longer our first love. We are content in our unrighteousness (sin). We are no longer walking the straight and narrow path to Heaven, but have meandered onto the broad and wide path to Hell. We are no longer living for Christ. Our life is centered upon self and what it desires or enjoys.

Because of this, we just sit by and allow ourselves to be influenced by the ungodliness and unrighteousness around us. We no longer believe our birth or biological sex is what we are, but we can choose our sex. God from the beginning of creation made us

Apathetic Indifference

male and female (Mark 10:6). We no longer believe that lying with mankind as with womankind (homosexuality) is an abomination to God (Leviticus 18:22). Instead of proclaiming biblical truth that will set those living is such sins free, we listen to the false teachers telling us we are doing harm to the homosexuals, transgenders, and religious people alike and sit idly by as they slip into Hell.

Why is there such a lack of righteousness in those claiming to belong to Christ? Why are we more concerned about hurt feelings than eternity? When will we love people enough to tell them the truth? When will we hate the garments defiled by the flesh and pull them out of the fire? When will we comprehend that only as we do righteousness are we born of him? When will we realize that if we do not warn of sin, God will require their blood at our hand? (Ezekiel 3:18)

If we are not doing what pleases God, we are, in fact doing what pleases self. We are not to fellowship with what is contrary to God's word. Yet how many are heaping to themselves false ministers? Instead of fighting the good fight of faith, most are seeking to hear sinful indulgence is accepted by God. After all, a God of love will never send us to Hell.

> *4)So that we ourselves glory in you in the churches of God for your patience and faith in all your persecutions and tribulations that ye endure: 5)Which is a manifest token of the righteous judgment of God, that ye may be counted worthy of the kingdom of God, for which ye also suffer: 6)Seeing it is a righteous thing with God to recompense tribulation to them that trouble you; 7)And to you who are troubled rest with us, when the Lord Jesus shall be revealed from heaven with his mighty angels, 8)In flaming fire taking vengeance on them that know not God, and that obey not the gospel of our Lord Jesus Christ: 9)Who shall be punished with everlasting destruction from the presence of the Lord, and from the glory of his power; 10)When he shall come to be glorified in his saints, and to be admired in all them that believe (because our testimony among you was believed) in that day. 11)Wherefore also we pray always for you, that our God would count you worthy of this calling, and fulfil all the good pleasure of his goodness, and*

> *the work of faith with power. 12)That the name of our Lord Jesus Christ may be glorified in you, and ye in him, according to the grace of our God and the Lord Jesus Christ. (2 Thessalonians 1:4–12)*

Scripture is clear Christ is coming back, and He will severely punish sin. The apathetic indifference for righteousness in those claiming to be Christians will find themselves being the recipients of his flaming fire or the recompense of all who lived in unrighteousness.

> *He that saith, I* know *him, and keepeth not his commandments, is a liar, and the truth is not in him. (1 John 2:4)*

We cannot claim to know Christ and live in sin. Our keeping his word reveals the truth is in us and we know him. Our not keeping his commandments (his word) reveals the truth is not in us and we do not know him. We may say we know him, but if we do not keep his word, we are a liar.

When Paul states Christ is coming back in flaming fire to take vengeance on those who obey not the gospel, he is also talking about those claiming to be Christians who are not keeping the word of God. Christ makes clear if there is no repentance, He will vomit all who are lukewarm out of his mouth (Revelation 3:16).

Christ is coming back for a righteous people, not a people who have indulged in unrighteous living and have encouraged unrighteousness in others. We cannot expect to be rewarded for our lack of self-denial, our lack of fighting the good fight of faith, or our lack of running the race set before with steadfast perseverance.

How many of us sit and watch ungodly television shows, movies, etc.? How many of us compromise with the sins of pornography, fornication, adultery, homosexuality, lies, gossip, and other corruption? How many of us have left the race to live for this life and ignore eternity?

Whereas, if we would keep our focus on eternity, we would fight the good fight of faith, stay out of the bleachers, and run the race set before us with resoluteness. We would fight all unrighteousness, ungodliness, and unholiness and give it no place.

Apathetic Indifference

How many times have we seen Christians with a zeal to fight the good fight of faith at first? There is a genuine fervor for Christ, but we will not let go of a little leaven. Before long, the corruption spreads and spreads until debasement has caused us to no longer run the race set before us. We live in apathetic indifference until we stop living a righteous life.

It is essential for God's soldiers to have a fervor for righteousness. Without it, we will not fight the good fight of faith. We need to be consecrated to him and to be separated from this world. If we have an eagerness for righteousness, godliness, and holiness, we will shun the so-called pleasures of this world with its corruption of the soul and run our race with patience.

When Jesus walked this earth, He was the self-revelation of God the Father. We, as the children of God, should be a self-revelation of Jesus in and through our lives. Many of us lack a dedication to Christ that fights the good fight of faith. Therefore, most are a self-revelation of the flesh.

That is a hard saying, but only truth will set us free from our apathetic indifference or lack of zeal and help us get back in the race and fight the good fight of faith. Our Scripture text in 1 John 2:29 is quite clear that only as we do righteousness are we born of him. We cannot live in unrighteousness and believe we are born of God.

1 Corinthians 15:33-34 warns us to not be deceived into thinking evil communications will not corrupt us. Many who are actually born of God have lost their passion for the things of God, have become lukewarm, are in a serious state of deception, and are about to be overcome by unbelief through apathetic indifference.

There are so few living a righteous life. Sitting in the pews with the lukewarm Christians, listening to their evil communications, and fellowshipping with them, has corrupted what was a separated life. Remember a little leaven will leaven or corrupt the whole (Galatians 5:9).

If God's soldiers were hearing about the dangers of losing their zeal to fight the good fight of faith and their desire to run the race with patience from the pulpit, there would be an awareness to avoid it. The truth is not preached from many pulpits, and it definitely is not being taught by those living in apathetic indifference.

We are either for Christ or we are against him. Being eighty, ninety, or even ninety-nine percent for Christ will give place to the anti-Christ spirit. If we are not one-hundred percent for Jesus, we give place to the devil to deceive.

We cannot allow deception to be planted in our mind. Only as we fight the good fight of faith, run the race set before us with patience, will we overcome and inherit all things. Because the gap between the world and those with an apathetic indifference is closing up, we cannot permit any disloyalty to distract us from our goal.

> *26)For if we sin willfully after that we have received the knowledge of the truth, there remaineth no more sacrifice for sins, 27)But a certain fearful looking for of judgment and fiery indignation, which shall devour the adversaries. 28)He that despised Moses' law died without mercy under two or three witnesses: 29)Of how much sorer punishment, suppose ye, shall he be thought worthy, who hath trodden under foot the Son of God, and hath counted the blood of the covenant, wherewith he was sanctified, an unholy thing, and hath done despite unto the Spirit of grace? (Hebrews 10:26-29)*

If God's soldiers continue to be seduced and seduced by the false ministers, the evil communications around, the corruption of the world, there will be no fighting the good fight of faith. It will be apostasy that awaits God's judgment. If we do despite the Spirit of grace, we willfully rebel against the Holy Spirit. Ignoring the conviction of the Spirit will lead to the death of enthusiasm to run our race. Without running the race set before us, there is no finishing.

One of the problems for this decline in passion is the church today is a replica of the Corinthian Church. We are born-again, baptized in the Holy Spirit, flowing in the gifts, but living like the devil. A sinner's prayer and flowing in the gifts does not insure our finishing the race. It is a life of self-denial that takes up our cross daily that will continue to fight the good fight of faith and run our race to the finish line.

APATHETIC INDIFFERENCE

Christian, awake to righteousness. Get out of the bed of lethargy. Get out of the seat of complacency. We are sleeping while souls are on a greased-pole to Hell. Furthermore, much of the church is dying spiritually and in complete ignorance of what is happening. If there is no repentance from apathetic indifference, we will become twice dead (Jude 1:12).

The consuming fire, the refiners fire is not burning in most anymore. The fact that apathetic indifference has risen in the body of Christ exposes the absence of the Holy Spirit and fire cleansing process. When the passion is consuming, it will condemn all unrighteousness in our life. It will give the desire to separate from the world. We will fight the good fight of faith and be severed from all that is unholy and ungodly.

God wants us to have a fervor for righteousness. He wants us to be so impassioned for godliness and righteousness that we shake up the enemy's ocean of unrighteousness, ocean of ungodliness, ocean of evil. We need a knowledge of the word that will enable us to go forth wise as serpents and as harmless as doves. We will seem like innocent doves while making surges in the ocean of Satan's power.

Because apathetic indifference is becoming so great, those who have an active and living zeal for righteousness will recognize the wheat and tares in the church. As we fight the good fight of faith, we will know our lives are upsetting their evil lives because we will be persecuted, ridiculed, mocked, called haters, bigots, etc.

Christ is coming back, and He will destroy all who do not obey his word. Too many are deceived into thinking Jesus will not destroy believers who said the sinner's prayer. Because we have neglected to awake to righteous living, have become hearers only and not doers of the word, and are committing the sins that will not inherit the kingdom of God, we will be the recipients of the flaming fire and fiery indignation of the Lord's judgment.

Many claim a God of love, yet forget the God of justice who will take vengeance on those who do not know God and **obey** not the gospel of Christ. We are liars if we claim to know him and do not keep his commandments (1 John 2:4). God does not condone sin. He is a righteous and holy God. The church of compromise or apathetic indifference is not portraying a righteous God. Such acquiescence has quenched the knowledge of God in our lives and in the lives we associate with. We have quit fighting the good fight of faith against sin. We are not running our race, but are content to sit in the bleachers.

Apathetic indifference will be toppled over by its own sin. Sin in lives will consume and destroy. Once we recognize this truth, it will cause us to fight the good fight of faith, separate ourselves from lukewarm teachings, compromising teachings, sinful practices, and make a difference.

As the early church stood against sin at the peril of their life, when is today's church going to stand up for Christ no matter what? When are we going to be so zealous for righteousness that we will be prepared to lose our life for God?

As the passion for righteousness is burning in us, it is going to come out in our speech, in our actions, and in every aspect of our lives. Because righteousness is opposite of unrighteousness, it will burn inside us with a intensity that consumes all ungodliness before it can become corruption in our life.

We will make those who are deceived in their apathetic indifference uncomfortable. We will cause those who are deceived by sin squirm and not even know why. A dynamic passion for the things of God is not lifeless. It fights the good fight of faith and runs the race with resolute perseverance until it finishes!

Chapter 7

Walk in the Spirit

If we live in the Spirit, let us also walk in the Spirit (Galatians 5:25).

This I say then, Walk in the Spirit, and ye shall not fulfil the lust of the flesh (Galatians 5:16).

WALKING IN THE SPIRIT seems like a simple admonition or command, but many of God's soldiers have no idea what it means to walk in the Spirit. Yet, the apostle Paul makes clear that only as we walk in the Spirit will we not fulfil the lust of our flesh.

What does it mean to walk in the Spirit? It means we deny self, our flesh, our carnal nature any foothold in our life. We must give it no place to influence our thought process. If we are to walk in the Spirit, we must allow the cleansing fire of the Holy Spirit to work in our life and allow him to do the work God sent him to do.

We cannot fight the good fight of faith nor run the race set before us with determined persistence in our carnal nature. Only in the Spirit can we overcome the lust of the flesh, the lust of the eyes, and the pride of life that are obstacles meant to stray us from the straight and narrow.

Unless we fully allow the Holy Spirit to guide us, we will be diverted from the fight and the race. We need to cultivate an intimate relationship with the Spirit of God. We tend to forget He is the one who dwells within us. He is here to help us live a Christ-like life. It was the Holy Spirit who led Jesus to live an overcoming life of faith. He overcame all He encountered here, and was given strength through faith to suffer the cross.

> *So then they that are in the flesh cannot please God. (Romans 8:8)*

Walking in the Spirit is the only way to keep us from yielding to our flesh. Jesus revealed He did not allow his flesh to control any part of his life. He fought the good fight of faith and ran the race set before him which enabled him to walk constantly in the Spirit, thereby allowing him to please the Father in all things. Unless we are walking in the Spirit, we cannot please the Father. If we are not walking under the guidance and direction of the Holy Spirit, we are walking under the guidance and direction of the flesh. If we are in the flesh, we cannot please God.

> *19)What? know ye not that your body is the temple of the Holy Ghost which is in you, which ye have of God, and ye are not your own? 20)For ye are bought with a price: therefore glorify God in your body, and in your spirit, which are God's (1 Corinthians 6:19-20).*

God's soldiers do not belong to themselves. Once we are born again, we are to give ourselves freely to the Holy Spirit to do God's will in our life. Although He lives or resides in our spirits, his work is limited by what we allow him to do. We are free-will beings who can choose to be led by the Spirit of God or ignore his promptings and be led by our flesh.

That is why we must die to self or our old nature and oblige him to achieve God's purpose in our lives. Our carnal mind is in opposition to the mind of Christ and must be renewed by the Holy Spirit to think his thoughts (Romans 12:2; Philippians 2:5).

If we are going to walk in the Spirit, He has to be permitted to teach us spiritual discernment. Unless the Holy Spirit is leading us, we will not discern the difference between the Holy Spirit, the flesh, or an evil spirit influencing us. Only He can help us recognize what is good and evil, what is of God, and what is not of God. How can we walk with him if we cannot discern what is righteous from what is unrighteous? How can we walk with him if we cannot discern truth from lies?

As we yield to the Holy Spirit, He will put a warning in our minds that what we have heard is not quite right. We feel this inward check that something is wrong. Because of those restraints, we are kept from stumbling.

> 12)*Let not sin therefore reign in your mortal body, that ye should obey it in the lusts thereof.* 13)*Neither yield ye your members as instruments of unrighteousness unto sin: but yield yourselves unto God, as those that are alive from the dead, and your members as instruments of righteousness unto God.* 14)*For sin shall not have dominion over you: for ye are not under the law, but under grace (Romans 6:12-14).*

Because Christ has set us free from the power of sin (John 8:36), it no longer has rule over us. The above Scripture exposes sin tries to reign in us through the desires and lusts of our body or our old nature. We are the ones who decide to yield or not to yield to unrighteousness. Sin does NOT have dominion over us. Through the blood of Christ, we have the power over sin. He has given us the power to fight the good fight of faith, run our race with patience, and overcome all the power of Satan.

Sin has no power over us unless we yield to it. This means we relinquish our authority over all of Satan's power and choose to yield to sin. Surrendering to sin means we have willingly forfeited our authority over Satan to him.

The Holy Spirit came to deliver us from all the dominion of sin. Whenever we are walking in our flesh, we are not walking in the Spirit. If we are not walking in the Spirit, the Holy Spirit is not leading our life. If the Holy Spirit is not leading our life, we will give into the flesh's desire to sin.

As the temple of the Holy Spirit, we are the dwelling place for the essence of holiness. We must not allow our bodies to be defiled by impurity or evil whether in our actions, our thoughts, our desires, our words, etc. God's Spirit came to make our temple a place of victory over sin. To have the victory, we must walk in the Spirit. We cannot fight the good fight of faith or run the race set before us with tenacity in the flesh. Because the flesh is focused upon its lusts, it will never deny self what it wants.

I am not claiming that we will never sin again. What I am claiming is that sin does not have to control us. If we yield to the flesh, we will always sin. However, as we yield to the Holy Spirit, He delivers us from sin. He that is born of God cannot sin (1 John 3:9). When we yield to the Spirit, He changes our desires, so we do not want to live the way we did when sin had control over us. Once the Holy Spirit is influencing our desires, He enables us to hate the things God hates.

As a young Christian, the pastor, of the church I attended, preached a sermon that I have never forgotten. He said that he smokes as much as he wants, he fornicates as much as he wants, he gets drunk as much as he wants to, etc. I remember sitting there with my eyes widened and my mouth opened at his words. Then, he said the difference is that the Holy Spirit took the **"want to"** out of his life. That truth sums up being led by the Holy Spirit and not self or the flesh.

> *The Spirit of the Lord is upon me, because he hath anointed me to preach the gospel to the poor; he hath sent me to heal the brokenhearted, to preach deliverance to the captives, and recovering of sight to the blind, to set at liberty them that are bruised (Luke 4:18).*

The anointing Jesus is speaking of is the Holy Spirit. It is an inner anointing now dwelling within us who are born again. It is a healing of the Holy Spirit set up inside us to bring healing to the whole man. It brings spiritual healing to our souls, heals our physical distresses, brings divine help to our minds, and any part of us that has been injured or bruised. In whatever way we have been wounded, whether spiritually, physically, mentally, or emotionally,

He has our healing. He is our healing for whatever we may have suffered, have experienced in our life or may be suffering or experiencing at present.

We must not allow self-pity over emotional injuries as an excuse for our present failures. If we have not experienced his healing in certain areas of our lives, perhaps we refuse to forgive. We need to yield to his love and power to free us from the effects of whatever is stifling our healing.

As we yield to the Holy Spirit in us, we can overcome our old nature which is prone to sin and grow in Christlikeness. We have to give up our lives to receive his. This takes place as we exchange our old nature at the cross, choosing to die to its sinful ways, and receiving his life. We do this by choosing to decrease and allowing him to increase (John 3:30).

As we decrease and He increases, we walk less in the flesh and more in the Spirit. Through this Christlikeness, we will experience overcoming faith displayed in a greater way in our life. As we walk in the Spirit, He gives us the divine enablement to fight the good fight of faith and the fortitude to run our race with patience until the end!

Chapter 8

Suffering And Gethsemane

36)Then cometh Jesus with them unto a place called Gethsemane, and saith unto the Disciples, Sit ye here, while I go and pray yonder. 37)And he took with him Peter and the two sons of Zebedee, and began to be sorrowful and very heavy. 38)Then saith he unto them, My soul is exceeding sorrowful, even unto death: tarry ye here, and watch with me. 39)And he went a little farther, and fell on his face, and prayed, saying, O my Father, if it be possible, let this cup pass from me: nevertheless not as I will, but as thou wilt. (Matthew 26:36-39)

For unto you it is given in the behalf of Christ, not only to believe on him, but also to suffer for his sake (Philippians 1:29)

GETHSEMANE MEANS WINE PRESS or a place of mental or spiritual suffering. Although chapter three revealed suffering is something we all partake of, this chapter is meant to illuminate that

Suffering And Gethsemane

suffering and service go hand in hand for the disciples of Christ. If we believe once we are saved we have a life free of struggles, we will never cultivate the perseverance to fight the good fight of faith and run the race set before us to the finish. That is why many fell by the wayside from the prosperity preachers who promised if we come to Christ, our financial troubles are a thing of the past.

We cannot be in the Lord's service without partaking of his suffering in this life and partaking of Gethsemane at the end. If we are to endure Gethsemane, our faith is not fortified on the mountain top. It is in the valley of trials, storms, hardships, griefs, etc. that the perseverance to continue the fight and finish the race is nurtured.

Unless we comprehend our life must share in Christ's sufferings, we will never endure Gethsemane. Prayerfully this chapter will encourage us to persevere through all trials and be prepared to go through Gethsemane before we complete our race.

> 6)Wherein ye greatly rejoice, though now for a season, if need be, ye are in heaviness through manifold temptations:7) That the trial of your faith, being much more precious than of gold that perisheth, though it be tried with fire, might be found unto praise and honour and glory at the appearing of Jesus Christ (1 Peter 1:6–7).

It is imperative as we go through the trials or sufferings of this life that we do not become discouraged because of the difficulties. As we remain faithful to Christ during the times where the purifying fire is turned up, our faith will be refined as pure gold. Having our faith purified will result in the stamina that fights the good fight of faith with perseverance and runs the race set before us with fortitude.

The encouraging part of the refiner's fire is our faith is far more valuable than pure gold. When we come through, our faith gives praise, honor, and glory to God. The **point** is that we must come through, persevere, or endure if our faith is to glorify God.

> 12)Beloved, think it not strange concerning the fiery trial which is to try you, as though some strange thing happened unto you: 13)But rejoice, inasmuch as ye are partakers of

Christ's sufferings; that, when his glory shall be revealed, ye may be glad also with exceeding joy (1 Peter 4:12–13).

As Christians, we should expect fiery trials. Scripture makes evident that suffering is an inevitable part of our life. Yet, so many of us react as if something alien is happening when we are faced with troubles, difficulties, suffering, grief, etc.

Sharing in Christ's sufferings is the only way to develop the tenacity that endures the fight and overcomes the fiery trials trying to destroy us. When Christ returns, we will be overjoyed because as we partook of his sufferings here, we will partake of his glory there. It is imperative for us to perceive the reality of partaking of his sufferings. Without sharing in his sufferings in this life, there will be no partaking of his glory later.

It is through the sufferings we go through that enables God to form within us the quality of character necessary to mold us more into the image of Christ. If we persevere the increase of suffering, we will become strengthened in our resolve to fight the good fight of faith against sin and the devil. We will have the determination to run the race set before us no matter how many obstacles we must defeat or overcome.

> *3)And the Lord said unto Satan, Hast thou considered my servant Job, that there is none like him in the earth, a perfect and an upright man, one that feareth God, and escheweth evil . . . ? 4)And Satan answered the Lord, and said, Skin for skin, yea, all that a man hath will he give for his life. 5)But forth thine hand now, and touch his bone and his flesh, and he will curse thee to thy face. 6)And the Lord said unto Satan, Behold, he is in thine hand; but save his life. 7)So went Satan forth from the presence of the Lord, and smote Job with sore boils from the sole of his foot unto his crown, 8)And he took him a potsherd to scrape himself withal; and he sat down among the ashes (Job 2:3–8).*

The book of Job reveals suffering is a sign of devotion to God and proves fidelity to him does not equate exemption from suffering. Christians really need to receive the revelation that without the things we suffer, we will never develop the tenacity to continue fighting and to keep running.

We need to grasp that when our life pleases God, the devil is provoked. When he is incited, he will attack us from all angles. His motive is to destroy our faith. He wants us to quit the fight and leave the race. That is why it is imperative to know that pleasing God will result in suffering. With that truth, what could be more satisfying than to know our faith is so pleasing to God that we have angered the devil?

Like stated in chapter three, I realize all mankind grieves, faces sorrow associated with significant loss. Whether it is death, divorce, loss of a job, loss of a home, loss of a loved one, etc., suffering causes grief to all of mankind. However the Christian suffering is meant to strengthen our resolve to keep fighting. In the lost, it is to urge them to turn to Christ for help.

> 25)Jesus said unto her, I am the resurrection, and the life: he that believeth in me, though he were dead, yet shall he live:26)And whosoever liveth and believeth in me shall never die. Believest thou this? (John 11:25-26)

Christians have a foundation that makes our suffering different from the suffering of the lost. The knowledge that Christ rose from the dead, prepares the way for acceptance of the fact that we will be resurrected when the Lord returns. This realization enables us to have hope in the face of any suffering. Hope gives us strength to fight the good fight of faith and run our race with patience.

As God's soldiers, we believe we shall rise again, not disembodied, but clothed in a bodily form. But do we realize we shall rise again with our own body, in our very flesh? The only difference is we will be healed and immortal. Our body shall be deathless and glorious as the body of Jesus when He arose from the dead.

Do we understand what Jesus is promising in John 11:25-26? He is telling us this life and the life to come are not two lives, but one and the same. Death is not the ending of one and the resurrection the beginning of another. Through all, there runs one imperishable life. All who live and believe in him shall never die.

It is like a river that plunges into the earth and is buried for a while; then it bursts forth more mightily, and in a fuller tide. It is not two rivers, but one continuous stream. It is the same river buried in the earth only to come forth greater.

The light of today is not quenched at sunset and rekindled at sunrise tomorrow. It is one broad and luminous sun. Today's sun is the same sun that appeared yesterday and the same sun that will appear tomorrow. So it is with life and death. Our soul is immortal, an image of God's own eternity.

Few of us realize as we die, so shall we rise. As there is not a new beginning of our life, so there is no new beginning of our character. The stream which buries itself cloudy and corrupted shall rise clouded and corrupted. The waters which pass clear and bright into the earth shall rise from it clear and bright again.

Consecration is lacking in most Christians. We are not wholly devoted to God and His kingdom. Think about this. The time from planting to harvest takes time. It is a constant vigil to keep out weeds, critters, etc. That is why we must continuously endeavor to get the world and its pleasures out of us.

Our character determines how we will be resurrected (please note that we will all be resurrected to either life or condemnation). Our character is our will and what we will is who we are. Character is the total quality of our behavior, as revealed in our habits of thought and expression, our attitudes, our interests, our actions, our personal philosophy of life. It is what we are. Thus, what we will or choose is who we are. Our choices reveal what sort of character we possess.

Our will contains our whole intention and sums up our spiritual nature. Our soul bent on rebellion against God's word here will break forth then into the full measure of its spiritual malice. If it dies unrighteous, it will resurrect in full unrighteousness. Whereas our soul bent on consecrating itself wholly to God and obeying his word will break forth into the full measure of spiritual sanctity. If our soul dies righteous, it will resurrect in full righteousness.

In other words, whatever we are endeavoring to be here, we will be the fullness of it in the resurrection. We will either resurrect holy or we will resurrect wicked. What we are here is what we will be then. If we have pursued righteousness, we will come forth unto the resurrection of life. If we have pursued unrighteousness, we will be part of the resurrection of condemnation (John 8:29).

If that truth does not convince us to strive to live a life wholly consecrated to God, we are in a sad state. For such knowledge should encourage us to delete anything in our life that could displease God. It should cause a revival of holiness in those claiming to belong to Christ.

We need to comprehend that if we do not go through the sufferings, we will not cultivate the tenacity to fight the good fight of faith nor run the race set before us with patience. Without suffering, we will not learn obedience. Without obedience, we will not be part of the resurrection of life.

Let me interject a truth that is the foundation for our continuing to fight the good fight of faith and to run the race set before us with patience. The root of our persisting is based upon desire. What is the desire of our heart? Do we desire to be with the Lord? Do we desire to spend eternity with him? Do we desire to be part of the resurrection of life? Do we desire to be righteous, holy, and godly?

Our desire will reveal our willingness to suffer in this life to achieve that desire. We will not be like those who want the easy life, we will willingly suffer for our desire. This life is not our goal. We are looking for that city which has foundations whose builder and maker is God.

Christ's desire was to set us free from sin and allow us to fellowship with God. His heart's desire was our good. He gave no place to his flesh and willingly suffered to bring about our salvation. His suffering was for us. All Christ endured, the pain and agony, was out of love for us.

If our desire is him, we will choose to suffer for him. The early martyrs gave their lives for the faith. Their desire was to overcome this life and enter eternity with Christ. Only as our desire for him is above all else will we comprehend that it is given in the behalf of Christ, not only believe on him, but to willingly suffer for his sake (Philippians 1:29).

All of us will be resurrected either to the resurrection of life or the resurrection of death. Whatever our character has been here is what it will be there. If it has not strived to be holy, righteous, and godly like Christ, it will not be such in the hereafter. Once we comprehend all of us will be resurrected either to eternal life or to eternal damnation, it causes us to reevaluate our life and **desire** to change whatever is necessary to walk in righteousness.

It is time for us who claim to be Christians to consider wholeheartedly which resurrection we are conforming our character to. Christ learned obedience by the things He suffered (Hebrews 5:8). He fought the good fight of faith and ran the race set before him by denying his flesh and giving it no place in his life.

As we learn to share in Christ's suffering in our daily life, we will be preparing ourselves to partake of Gethsemane. The Mount of Olives is where Jesus went to pray before his death.

We know his soul was extremely sorrowful before his death. He was not suffering to go to the cross or to die, but his death meant being separated from his Father for the first time since eternity. In order for Jesus to become our sin, a holy God could not look upon such and must turn away.

The objective of this chapter is not about what Jesus suffered at Gethsemane. We need to comprehend that before our death, we will have to go through the wine press. Why do I say that? I believe we must all face our death.

Will we willingly accept that our race is finished? Will our heart be so tied to our loved ones that we do not want to leave? Will we claim we are too young? Will we plead for more time or will we say *nevertheless not as I will, but as thou wilt*?

What we have been doing up to that point will determine how well we endure Gethsemane. If we have not readily accepted that suffering is our lot in this life if we are going to follow Christ, we will not accept Gethsemane.

In my book, *Satan's Strategy to Torment through Physical Ambush* is an example of willingly suffering for Christ and enduring Gethsemane. The martyrs were in their Gethsemane. They faced the lions den, burning at the stake, etc. Would they choose to die for Christ or would they choose to deny him?

> *And he said to them all, If any man will come after me, let him deny himself, and take up his cross daily, and follow me. (Luke 9:23)*

Unless we have truly comprehended what it means to follow Jesus, we will not understand that we must continue to fight the good fight of faith and run the race set before us with patience until we cross the finish line. Gethsemane is our last suffering.

Jesus was our example of self-denial. He willingly endured the suffering of his life and the suffering of Gethsemane for us to be with him. If we are to come after him, we must choose to partake of his sufferings in this life and suffer through Gethsemane to be with him.

Yes, Christians do not fear death. But how many are ready for it when the time comes? If all of a sudden, we find ourselves in Gethsemane (our time of death), will we struggle? How we have been living our life will determine whether we face Gethsemane grudgingly or enthusiastically.

Only as we live each day willingly choosing to partake in the sufferings of Christ will we willingly choose God's will and not ours in Gethsemane. This reality will keep us denying self, fighting the good fight of faith, and running our race with resolute fortitude knowing that after Gethsemane is the finish line!

Chapter 9

Champion Runner

> *30)And Caleb stilled the people before Moses, and said, Let us go up at once, and possess it; for we are well able to overcome it. 32)But the men that went up with him said, We be not able to go up against the people; for they are stronger than we. 32)And they brought up an evil report of the land which they had searched unto the children of Israel, saying, The land, through which we have gone to search it, is a land that eateth up the inhabitants thereof; and all the people that we saw in it are men of a great stature. 33)And there we saw the giants, the sons of Anak, which come of the giants: and we were in our own sight as grasshoppers, and so we were in their sight. (Numbers 13:30-33)*

WHAT IS A CHAMPION? It is a person that has defeated or surpassed all rivals. Whatever trial, test, obstacle, etc. comes the champion's way, he/she conquers them all. A champion runner overcomes all impediments of storms, trials, obstacles, grief, heartache and finishes the race victoriously.

Our champion runner will not be found in the faith chapter in the book of Hebrews. In order for us to comprehend what a champion is, we need to understand that it can be an ordinary person who possesses an extra-ordinary faith in God. It is someone like us, who by faith is enabled to run through unrivaled trials.

We do not hear much about Caleb, but he was a champion runner who fought the good fight of faith under incredible circumstances. He ran the race set before him with fortitude and determination that hurdled all obstacles. He trusted in God's faithfulness to keep his promises when many would have become weary with such a lengthy and grueling race.

We see in the scriptures above that he was ready to go in and possess the Promised Land at the first visit to Kadesh Barnea. However, the slanderous or evil report from the ten caused the people to believe them and not God. It is important to understand it was an evil report whose slanderous language was in fact against God. It was God's ability that was doubted. Their unbelief focused upon God Almighty.

> *But without faith it is impossible to please him: for he that cometh to God must believe that he is, and that he is a rewarder of them that diligently seek him. (Hebrews 11:6)*

The ten spies did not please God. Why not? Because of their slanderous report, they promoted unbelief in the people. Unbelief caused the people to see God as impotent or powerless. Yet these people had witnessed him perform such miracles like parting the Red Sea and enabling them to walk across on dry land, turning the bitter water into sweet, supplying manna six days a week, etc.

Faith believes that God is and that He is a rewarder of them that relentlessly seek him. Caleb believed in his God to deliver them according to his promise. He steadfastly fought the good fight of faith by running the race set before him with patience. Caleb was resolute and unmovable in his faith.

For faith to be complete, it must possess both components. It must believe God is and that God rewards faith in him. If we believe in God's existence without doubts and are certain that He exists, but doubt He rewards faith, we call God a liar. We fail in the faith component and displease God. To please God, we must possess both components of the faith that pleases him.

> *And I will give unto thee, and to thy seed after thee, the land wherein thou art a stranger, all the land of Canaan, for an everlasting possession. (Genesis 17:8)*

This is the land that God promised Abraham. God is not a man that He can lie (Numbers 23:19). But the unbelief of the ten leavened thousands of people to accept the lie. They rejected the word of God for them to possess it, and believed the evil report.

Unbelief kept many thousands from receiving the Promised Land. Instead they inherited the reaping of the sin of unbelief. All their carcasses fell in the wilderness because the evil report fostered unbelief instead of faith in the God who had delivered them with a mighty hand from the Egyptian bondage.

> *29)Your carcasses shall fall in this wilderness; and all that were numbered of you, according to your whole number, from twenty years old and upward which have murmured against me. 30)Doubtless ye shall not come into the land, concerning which I sware to make you dwell therein, save Caleb the son of Jephunneh, and Joshua the son of Nun. 34)After the number of the days in which ye searched the land, even forty days, each day for a year, shall ye bear your iniquities, even forty years, and ye shall know my breach of promise (Numbers 14:29-30,34)*

This people were at the door of the land God promised, but unbelief caused them to disobey. All they had to do was obey God and go in and possess it. The land was theirs for the taking, but instead they wandered in the wilderness for forty years until all over twenty died. Only Joshua and Caleb believed God, and at the end of the forty years, both inherited the land promised.

Instead of the people entering, the door was closed because of unbelief. They were punished to forty years of wandering like nomads with no place to call home. Unbelief caused all twenty and over to miss the land flowing with milk and honey. They did not fight the good fight of faith nor run the race set before them with patience. Instead, they just quit, and unbelief caused all twenty and over to miss God's promise land.

On the other hand, we saw Caleb was willing and ready to go in and possess the land, but the people believed the evil report. Now, the Lord punishes the people's lack of faith by causing them to wander in the wilderness for forty years until all guilty of unbelief died.

Only Joshua and Caleb would possess the land at the end of the forty years. It is imperative for us to bear in mind, they still had to wander in the wilderness for that length of time. Imagine being obedient to God, but the sin of the people caused Caleb to be a partaker in the penalty or punishment.

He had to wander with the murmurers and complainers for forty years. Can we even fathom walking side by side with the people who caused us to suffer or partake of their punishment for forty years? How many of us would have remained faithful and not fallen into complaining about our lot for obedience?

We start out at forty years of age and end the wandering at eighty. How many of us would have become a murmurer and complainer like the others after such an ordeal? How many of us would have become angry with God for causing us to be partakers of the punishment for being faithful? How many of us would have kept fighting the good fight of faith through it all? How many of us would have quit the race?

> *But my servant Caleb, because he had another spirit with him, and hath followed me fully, him will I bring into the land whereinto he went; and his seed shall possess it. (Numbers 14:24)*

Caleb never gave into the spirit of unbelief or doubt in God. He never complained about his lot. He never murmured against those who were guilty. Instead, he possessed the spirit of boldness, courage, and righteousness. He rose above the spirit of fear, the prompting of his flesh to complain, and followed God whole heartedly. In doing so, God was permitted to raise Caleb above human inquietudes. Because of faith, he enjoyed the peace of God that passes all understanding while he wandered in the desert all that time.

God had promised to bring Caleb into the land of promise and that his seed would possess it after him. Caleb wandered the wilderness the forty years with that promise bubbling inside him. He never wavered through incredible trials. His faith kept him seeing the promise as already visible.

> 9)And Moses sware on that day, saying, Surely the land whereon thy feet have trodden shall be thine inheritance, and thy children's for ever, because thou hast wholly followed the Lord my God. 10)And now, behold, the Lord hath kept me alive, as he said, these forty and five years, even since the Lord spake this word unto Moses, while the children of Israel wandered in the wilderness: and now, lo, I am this day fourscore and five years old. 11)As yet I am as strong this day as I was in the day that Moses sent me: as my strength was then, even so is my strength now, for war, both to go out, and to come in. (Joshua 14:9-11)

Caleb's faith never wavered during all those years, and God enabled him to go in and fight and possesses the land he was promised. His natural forces were just as strong at the age of eighty-five as it had been when he was sent in to spy the land at the age of forty.

That is the fortitude of a faith that pleases God. It believes God is and that God will reward if we do not waver in our faith. How many of us lose stamina through a difficulty after a week, a month, a year, five years, ten years?

If we are to become a champion runner, we need to consider Caleb. He is an example of what sort of race is set before us. Such runners fight the good fight of faith, run the race with perseverance, and victoriously cross the finish line!

Chapter 10

Spiritual Seeker

> 8)*Then the king of Syria warred against Israel, and took counsel with his servants, saying, In such and such a place shall be my camp. 9)And the man of God sent unto the king of Israel, saying, Beware that thou pass not such a place, for thither the Syrians are come down. 10)And the king of Israel sent to the place which the man of God told him and warned him of, and saved himself there, nor once nor twice. 11)Therefore the heart of the king of Syria was sore troubled for this thing; and he called his servants, and said unto them, Will ye not shew me which of us is for the king of Israel? 12)And one of his servants said, None, my lord, O king: but Elisha, the prophet that is in Israel, telleth the king of Israel the words that thou speakest in thy bedchamber.*
> (2 Kings 6:8–12)

ELISHA WAS A PROPHET who was a disciple and successor of Elijah. He was a spiritual seeker who possessed resolute steadfastness that is an example to all of God's soldiers. For this book, we are not going to focus upon Elijah. We are to keep our attention upon the faithfulness of Elisha in fighting the good fight of faith and running the race set before him with patience.

> 15)And the Lord said unto him, Go, return on thy way to the wilderness of Damascus: and when thou comest, anoint Hazael to be king over Syria: 16)And Jehu the son of Nimshi shalt thou anoint to be king over Israel: and Elisha the son of Shaphat of Abelmeholah shalt thou anoint to be prophet in thy room. 19)So departed thence, and found Elisha the son of Shaphat, who was plowing with twelve yoke of oxen before him, and he with the twelfth: and Elijah passed by him, and cast his mantle upon him. (1 Kings 19:15–16, 19)

There is no mention of Elisha until the verses above. All we know is that Elijah went northward and found Elisha plowing a field of his father's farm. When Elijah threw his mantle upon him, Elisha seemed to comprehend the symbolic act.

He realized Elijah was adopting him as a son and successor in the prophetic office. As Elijah strode on, Elisha, at first hesitated. But then he felt the irresistible force of the call of God and ran after the great prophet, announcing his readiness to follow. He became a spiritual seeker, making a full renunciation of home ties, comforts, and privileges to follow Elijah.

> 4)And Elijah said unto him, Elisha, tarry here, I pray thee; for the Lord hath sent me to Jericho. And he said, As the Lord liveth, and as thy soul liveth, I will not leave thee. So they came to Jericho. 5)And the sons of the prophets that were at Jericho came to Elisha, and said unto him, Knowest thou that the Lord will take away thy master from thy head to day? And he answered, Yea, I know it; hold ye your peace. 6)And Elijah said unto him, Tarry, I pray thee, here; for the Lord hath sent me to Jordan. And he said, As the Lord liveth, and as thy soul liveth, I will not leave thee. And they two went on. 7)And fifty men of the sons of the prophets went, and stood to view afar off: and they two stood by Jordan. 8)And Elijah took his mantle, and wrapped it together,

Spiritual Seeker

> and smote the waters, and they were divided hither and thither, so that they two went over on dry ground. 9)And it came to pass, when they were gone over, that Elijah said unto Elisha, Ask what I shall do for thee, before I be taken away from thee. And Elisha said, I pray thee, let a double portion of thy spirit be upon me. 10And he said, Thou has asked a hard thing: nevertheless, if thou see me when I am taken from thee, it shall be so unto thee; but if not, it shall not be so. 11)And it came to pass, as they still went on, and talked, that, behold, there appeared a chariot of fire, and horses of fire, and parted them both asunder; and Elijah went up by a whirlwind into heaven. 12)And Elisha saw it, and he cried, My faither, my faither, the chariot of Israel, and the horsemen thereof. And he saw him no more: and he took hold of his own clothes, and rent them in two pieces. 13)He took up also the mantle of Elijah that fell from him, and went back, and stood by the bank of Jordan. 14)And he took the mantle of Elijah that fell from him, and smote the waters, and said, Where is the Lord God of Elijah?and when he also had smitten the waters, they parted hither and thither: and Elisha went over. (2 Kings 2:4-14)

Nothing could dissuade Elisha from following the old prophet. He was aware Elijah's end was near at hand, and he determined to be with him until the last. We see Elisha would not be deterred from his fighting the good fight of faith nor from running his race with diligence. He was steadfast, unmoveable in his endeavor for the spiritual and not the physical or carnal.

When asked what Elijah should do for him, he asks for the elder son's portion, a double portion of his master's spirit. Elisha had no thought of equality. He would be Elijah's firstborn son.

Think of that. Elijah was not leaving him silver and gold or anything worldly. He was leaving Elisha a double portion of spiritual things. Do we comprehend what Elijah possessed was spiritual and that is what he was leaving to Elisha? The firstborn son's portion was double from what other sons would inherit.

May our children be spiritual seekers and so cherish the spiritual in us, that the double portion of the Spirit is all they desire to inherit. Do they witness us fighting the good fight of faith or do they see us doing the opposite? Do they observe us running the race set before us with patience or do they behold us living in stride with the world? Do they see us living for righteousness or unrighteousness? Do they hear us naming sin as sin or compromising sin? If we want those we love to crave the spiritual, we must be the example.

Let us continue with Elisha, the man of God. Elijah goes up in a whirlwind, and awestruck by the wonderful sight, Elisha rends his clothes. He then retraces his steps to the Jordan and smites the waters to test whether the Spirit of Elijah had really fallen upon him. He parts the water and passes over on dry ground.

We must comprehend that Elisha followed, obeyed, and was the servant of Elijah for years. 2 Kings 3:11 says, *Here is Elisha the son of Shaphat, which poured water on the hands of Elijah.* The verse reveals a servant and master relationship.

Elisha was a willing servant, as well as obedient. He could not expect the firstborn son's portion without loyalty to his father. That is an example to all who claim to be God's child. We will receive the firstborn son's portion (the portion of Jesus) ONLY through loyalty and obedience.

2 Kings 6 gives no explanation why there is a war going on. I believe God did not want us to focus upon the war. His objective was to have our attention concentrating upon Elisha, the man of God. Focusing upon the man of God causes us to focus upon the God of the man.

Only those with spiritual tunnel vision focus on the greatness of the man of God. Whereas those with spiritual peripheral vision see beyond the man to the God who empowers or endows him with his abilities. We comprehend that Elisha was a great man of God because of the great God of the man.

We look at Elisha or all the heroes of faith and think they are *"the untouchables."* We act as if there was something special about them. However, it is time to comprehend that the something special about them was their special God.

It is time for us to stop limiting God because our focus is on the heroes of the Bible. The previous chapter revealed Caleb was a hero because of his faith in God and in his ability to deliver upon his promises. The Lord wants us to see them, but not focus upon them. He wants us to look beyond them and focus upon him. He is the spiritual power behind them. Without God there would have been no supernatural power working in any of the heroes of faith.

If we are to fight the good fight of faith and run the race set before us with patience, we have to start focusing upon the HERO of the heroes of faith. It is not the heroes of the Bible who were omnipotent, omniscience, omnipresent, or immutable. It is the HERO of the heroes who is all-powerful, all-knowing, everywhere present, and unchangeable.

Unless we focus upon God, we will look at Elisha in our text and think what a special man of God he was. He was able to warn the king of Israel of every move of the Syrians before they moved. Each time the king of Syria was to camp in such and such a place, the man of God, Elisha, warned the king of Israel. He knew every move the ENEMY was going to make.

How did Elisha know that? Was he super smart? Was he an extra-ordinary human being? Of course not. It is God who is omniscient. It was God who gave Elisha a word of knowledge which is something known in the mind of God that pertains to persons, places, or things concerning the past or present. Elisha knew what God told him. It was not in Elisha's natural ability to know what was in the mind of God. Only God can reveal what is in his mind to his servants.

> *Lest Satan should get an advantage of us: for we are not ignorant of his devices. (2 Corinthians 2:11)*

If we are walking as one with God or walking in spirit and truth (John 4:24), we will be aware of the enemy's strategies. God will enable us to see (in the spirit) Satan's tactics. We will recognize how, when, and where he is moving. We will also see who he is working through.

As Elisha saw (spiritually) the moves of the enemy, so will any child of God who is walking in the spirit. God does not want us to be ignorant or unaware of Satan's devices (2 Corinthians 2:11). He wants us to recognize who is behind certain trials, circumstances, etc. in our life.

At present, many of us may have numerous stratagems coming against us. But as we remain spiritual seekers and align with God in the spirit, we recognize they are only pawns being moved and instigated by Satan and his demons.

It is imperative for us to keep fighting the good fight of faith and running our race with stamina. Satan knows if we are walking in the flesh, we are powerless against his diabolical schemes. Whereas in the spirit, we are more than conquerors through him that loves us (Romans 8:37).

What was the secret behind the power of Elisha? It was his steadfast determination to follow Elijah no matter what. He was a true spiritual seeker whose focus was upon the spiritual and not the physical. He stayed by Elijah's side even when the old prophet told him to remain behind.

How many of us are spiritual seekers who are so focused upon the spiritual that we will follow the Lord no matter what we may have to face in this life? How many of us become weary of the constant fight and the arduous race? What is our focus? Are we more occupied with receiving the spiritual blessings, or are we more engrossed with the comforts of this life?

Our life reveals where our focus is. If we are a physical seeker who indulges self and are living for the now, we will receive the inheritance without Christ. If we are spiritual seeker who denies self and are living for eternity, we will receive the inheritance with Christ.

Elisha knew how to deny himself, follow Elijah to the end, and receive his promised spiritual blessing. Spiritual seekers willingly deny self and follow Jesus until the finish. If we are a steadfast spiritual seeker who fights the good fight of faith and runs the race set before us with patience, we will overcome!

Chapter 11

No Distractions

6)Be careful for nothing; but in every thing by prayer and supplication with thanksgiving let your requests be made known unto God. 7)And the peace of God, which passeth all understanding, shall keep your hearts and minds through Christ Jesus. (Philippians 4:6–7)

WE CANNOT FIGHT THE good fight of faith nor run the race set before us with patience if we are distracted. If we are careful about things, we are anxious about them. We have distracting cares that will deter us from our endeavor to finish our race.

We were shown how to run without distractions by Caleb in chapter nine. His life reveals what sort of life we must be willing to live if we are to overcome and receive what God promises. Not many of us would have endured such a continuous race of endurance for forty years because of the sin of others.

How we become anxious or careful is through distraction. When we are distracted, our attention is diverted or drawn away from something to something else. This causes us to feel conflicting emotions. We are like a reed tossed to and fro. We saw that Caleb did not allow any distracting thoughts of his innocence and their guilt divert him from his race.

When we are anxious, our attention is turned from God and who He is to the distraction. It is plainly unbelief. Our God is able to keep our heart and mind through the worst of situations. If we are not kept, it is no fault of God. We have allowed our attention to be distracted.

The verse in Philippians is commanding us to have no distracting cares. When we do and we allow them to take control of our emotions, we will quit fighting the good fight of faith, and abandon our race. Our focus is no longer on our race but the distraction of finances, job, people, grief, etc.

Jesus told us we will have tribulation in this life (John 16:33), and we are to expect it. However, we are not supposed to allow the storms, obstacles, griefs, etc. of this life to overwhelm us with anxious care and distracting thoughts. We cannot permit them to redirect us from our fight of faith and finishing our race to the distraction.

It is imperative for us to be vigilant in heeding these verses, lest our anxiousness cause us to distrust God and give up like the Israelites in the wilderness. We **must** have no distractions if we are to finish the good fight of faith and run our race with patience.

These verses in Philippians not only give us a command against distracting thoughts or that which will lead us out of God's will, but it also gives the antidote, the remedy, the cure against anxiousness.

Verse seven tells us that no matter what is going on, we are to pray and supplicate with thanksgiving and let our requests be made known to God. We are to cry out to God in our distress. Because we know He is always with us, we expect, by faith, him to deliver us from all troubles.

The Lord knows anxiety cannot change the state or condition of anything from bad to good. As a matter of fact, it will cause bad to go to worse. Anxiety is unbelief or wavering. When we waver, we will not receive anything from the Lord (James 1:6–8).

> *13)Enter ye in at the strait gate: for wide is the gate, and broad is the way, that leadeth to destruction, and many there be which go in thereat: 14)Because strait is the gate, and narrow is the way, which leadeth unto life, and few there be that find it. (Matthew 7:13–14)*

Anxiousness is injurious to our soul. For when we are distracted, we stray from the straight and narrow which few find and merge onto the wide and broad that many enter in at. We go from fighting the good fight of faith and running the race set before us to joining those who live for self and not the Lord.

We must in every facet of our life pray to God. When anything burdens our spirit, we must ease our mind by prayer. Only as we commune with our God who gave his life for us to be in fellowship with him will we find peace of mind. The eye of the storm is only found in the presence of the Lord.

When our life is perplexed or distressed, we must seek direction and support. Our prayer is a solemn and humble application to God from a sense of need. Our supplication is a continuance in earnest prayer. Our heart is focused upon our God and not on the distraction.

What is prayer and supplication saying? It is our inner admission of our utter need, our complete dependence upon God, while also recognizing our unworthiness. This allows us to come to him with a sense of awe. As we humble ourselves in his sight, He will lift us up (James 4:10). He will give us the grace needed to continue fighting and running. His strength enables our weakness to do what it is not physically possible to do (2 Corinthians 12:9).

As stated in chapter three, we must always look up to God for help. When we are in distress, God is our only hope and our only help. He is promising in Philippians that if we cleave to him in times of trouble, He will keep our hearts and minds. He will replace our weakness with his strength. He will truly give us a peace of mind that transcends our understanding.

Too many of us run to people to talk to or to seek an answer instead of running to God. We allow the problem to distract us and turn aside to seek counsel from man. In doing so, we reap more troubles and woes. We are more overcome with anxiety and distress. Not all we may seek are led of the Spirit of God. Yes, we do receive counsel from godly men and women, but the perfect counsel for the troubled soul is the Holy Ghost. People can give physical comfort, but only God can give us the spiritual comfort our soul needs. Physical comfort will never reach into the troubled soul and deliver it from the inner pain.

It is the peace of God that will keep us from going under during the difficult times. Only He can help us overcome the hard times, the challenging times, the times of incredible grief, those times when it is beyond our understanding to comprehend. Once we realize that only God can console the heartache, grief, etc. we are suffering, will we supplicate him through prayer.

It is during the times of vulnerability that Philippians 4:6–7 must be engraved on our hearts and minds. We cannot allow the distraction of storms, heartache, difficulty, grief, etc. hinder us from fighting the good fight of faith and halt us from running our race.

When Satan comes in like a flood, the Spirit of the Lord shall lift up a standard against him (Isaiah 59:19b). The Holy Ghost will bring to our mind the scripture necessary to enable us to overcome and defeat the distraction. His word is a wall against the floods that will try to distract and engulf us.

We saw this truth with Caleb. Surely he was bombarded by the enemy during those forty years. But Caleb kept the promise of God steadfast in his heart. He believed God would keep him alive to possess the land and his seed after him.

There will be times that we will be sifted as wheat. Only God can keep our souls in safety against the assaults of Satan. Our affections and our reason must be kept in order, so that through Christ, we will not stop fighting nor quit running.

When all Hell breaks loose in our life to destroy our very foundation, cleaving to God, hanging onto him for dear life, will allow him to put our heart and mind in a strong place. His peace is the opposite of human anxiety.

Distractions are to prevent us from calling on God with a heart fully devoted to Christ. If we are focused upon the distraction, whatever it may be, we are not fixated upon our God. We will become like the Israelites who forgot the power, the greatness, the ability, etc. of God to deliver from whatever giant we must face.

> *Let us therefore come boldly unto the throne of grace, that we may obtain mercy, and find grace to help in time of need. (Hebrews 4:16)*

Through prayer, God promises to give us mercy and grace to help in time of need. When we commit our worries, grief, cares, etc. to God in prayer, his peace that passes all understanding will stand guard at the door of our hearts and minds. This will prevent any distraction from causing us to cease fighting the good fight of faith or prevent our running the race set before us with patience!

Chapter 12

Aggressive Warfare

1)Forasmuch then as Christ hath suffered for us in the flesh, arm yourselves likewise with the same mind: for he that hath suffered in the flesh hath ceased from sin; 2)That he no longer should live the rest of his time in the flesh to the lusts of men, but to the will of God.
(1 Peter 4:1–2)

SUFFERED MEANS TO EXPERIENCE a sensation (usually painful). It is to feel, to hurt, to agonize. Suffering is the state of undergoing pain, misery, agony, distress, or hardship. It implies being in great physical or mental strain and stress.

What Peter is relaying to us is that Christ suffered for doing good. Likewise, we are to be willing to suffer and should expect suffering for doing God's will. We should expect times of pain, misery, distress, and being in physical or mental stress as we follow Christ.

If we do not comprehend the necessity of equipping or arming our mind to do offensive (aggressive warlike attacking) warfare

Aggressive Warfare

like Jesus did to live a sinless life and go to the cross, we will never fight the good fight of faith nor run the race set before us with patience. This chapter is meant to illuminate that we must do aggressive/offensive warfare against the enemy if we are going to victoriously cross the finish line.

In defensive warfare, we guard, we stand unmoveable as the opponent comes at us. But offensive warfare means we are the aggressor, the attacker, the antagonist. We are the ones calling the shots. It is time for us to quit being on the defensive with the enemy and become the aggressor pushing the gates of Hell back.

> *And from the days of John the Baptist until now the kingdom of heaven suffereth violence, and the violent take it by force. (Matthew 11:12)*

The kingdom of God has suffered violence as demonic forces come against it and try to seize it up to this present time. We must be the violent (the aggressor) who take the kingdom of heaven by force. We must not allow anything to hinder our determination to prevent the powers of Hell from gaining any ground.

To be violent means to be a force, a power, energetic, strong, or potent. It means to possess a steadfast perseverance no matter what we are facing. It means to press forward with resolve that cannot be extinguished. It means to run the race set before us with relentless tenacity.

We are to equip ourselves with the same mind, thinking, or understanding as Christ. For he that has suffered in the flesh (human nature) has ceased, restrained from sin. Sin is contrary to God's will. To sin means we have chosen to step outside the boundaries God has set for us to follow. It is like the child who knows not to take without asking and takes it anyway. He/she has stepped outside of the boundaries set by the parent. We cannot sin without choosing to do so.

If we are not living to the will of God, we are living our life in the flesh or fulfilling the lusts of our carnal nature. The lusts of men is a longing or desire for what is forbidden by God. We are not to live for self-pleasure, but the purpose, the desire, the pleasure of God.

> 6)*And the Lord said unto Cain, Why art thou wroth? and why is thy countenance fallen? 7)If thou doest well, shalt thou not be accepted? and if thou doest not well, sin lieth at the door. And unto thee shall be his desire, and thou shalt rule over him. (Genesis 4: 6–7)*

In the verses in Genesis, God was revealing to Cain, and to us, that sin crouches at the door of our heart, watching and waiting to pounce us the moment we give it place. When we give place to sin, it will rule over us. Our carnal nature has no power over the temptation of sin. Only the spirit which is born of God will not sin (1 John 5:18). As we walk in the spirit, we have power over sin's control. Because of God's grace, sin no longer has dominion or control over us (Romans 6:14).

Cain was given every opportunity to do God's will, but he refused to put his flesh under, to suffer in his human nature to do God's pleasure. Instead of fighting the good fight of faith or running the race that would have enabled him to overcome, he blamed his brother for God's rejection of his offering. Because Cain refused to do aggressive warfare against his flesh and the enemy, he was overtaken by sin.

Genesis 4:5 reveals God had no respect **unto** Cain and his offering. It was not the offering God rejected, it was the condition of Cain's heart. There was sin in Cain's heart that had to be repented of. Instead of humbling himself before God, he killed his brother.

Let us try to understand what God wants us to see in this chapter. In order for us to cease, refrain, or stop sinning, we have to suffer in our flesh, our old nature, our human nature, our carnal nature. However, we cannot refrain without first equipping ourselves with the same mind, moral understanding, or thinking of Christ which is the will of God. The only way we can know the will of God, the boundaries He has set for us to follow, is through a knowledge of his word.

Aggressive Warfare

Study to shew thyself approved unto God, a workman that needeth not to be ashamed, rightly dividing the word of truth. (2 Timothy 2:15)

Knowing the Word of God enables us to have the boldness to do aggressive warfare (on offense) against sin. Cain permitted the sin lying at the door of his heart to seize him. But if he had done what was right in God's eye and violently took control of his flesh and gave no place to sin, he would not have lived the rest of his time to his carnal desires but to the will of God.

If we are to fight the good fight of faith and run the race set before us with patience, we have to do aggressive warfare against sin, against our human nature, against the devil. We have to take authority, be the strong force over any fleshly appetites or desires. It is a fight that must be fought daily. There is no relenting of the devil's attacks, and there must never be any conceding on our part to quit being aggressive against the enemy. Any compromise on our part will be detrimental to our overcoming.

Let me insert something here about the pull of sin and its corruptness. I dreamed that my husband and I were in this strange house. As we stepped out the door, there was a three-foot or so cement walk surrounding the house. All around the walkway was water that I thought was an ocean. I looked out at the horizon and saw only water with no land in sight. As Paul walked closer to take a swim, he suddenly jumped back. I then saw the water was black and putrid with all these people swimming just under the surface like it was pleasant. As we stood watching in bewilderment, the Lord told me it is the ocean of sin all around like the swamp of corruption in our government. He said anything other than his will and obedience to his word is the ocean of sin. The pull is great and many because of the lust of the flesh, the lust of the eyes, and the pride of life are jumping in. There is no thought for eternity, but the pleasures of this life.

We do not choose to fight one day and take a sabbatical the next or we will be seduced by the sin around. Jesus made clear that to follow him, we are to take up our cross of self-denial daily (Luke 9:23). Daily signifies without ceasing. It is never-ending as long as we are in this life. That is why it is a fight and a race. There is no stopping until we have fought the good fight of faith and have finished the race with patience.

> *Strive to enter in at the strait gate: for many, I say unto you, will seek to enter in, and shall not be able. (Luke 13:24)*

To strive to enter requires great effort. It implies to struggle or fight vigorously. Striving means to struggle in opposition, to contend. It takes offensive warfare to fight against that which could cause us to be distracted from fighting the good fight of faith and running the race set before us with persistent fortitude.

If we desire to be part of the kingdom of God, we will have to seize it by force. We must be the aggressor, the forcer against the violent, the sin, the distraction, the seizer trying to stop us. The enemy of the cross is constantly, violently trying to stop us from entering the kingdom or partaking of God's promises.

In Pilgrim's Progress, the devil tried to steer Pilgrim or Christian from the right path by the flatterer, worldly wiseman, etc. Because of distractions from the straight gate, Pilgrim found himself in the slough of despond, in Giant Despair's castle, and when trying to get to the gate, he was attacked by fiery arrows.

That is why we must know the Word of God, so we can think like Jesus. Being like Christ causes us to fight the good fight of faith, run the race, and become the aggressor, the overcomer, the seizer. Because we have learned to do offensive warfare, we do not allow sin to reign in our mortal body that we should obey its lusts (Romans 6:12).

> *For the flesh lusteth against the Spirit, and the Spirit against the flesh: and these are contrary the one to the other. (Galatians 5:17)*

Cain allowed jealousy of his brother and his anger at God to control his heart. Instead of leaning to God, he leaned on his understanding, and the devil or sin seized him. If he would have accepted his wrong doing as sin, repented, and turned to God, he would have become the aggressor and overcome.

Aggressive Warfare

> *Blessed is the man that endureth temptation: for when he is tried, he shall receive the crown of life, which the Lord hath promised to them that love him. (James 1:12)*

If we have read through this book, prayerfully, we have gained an understanding of the fight and the race we must endure. We comprehend the necessity to do aggressive warfare and that the forceful take the kingdom of God by spiritual, supernatural strength.

The verse in James reveals that if we persevere under trials, we will receive the crown of life. If we are to persevere in fighting the good fight of faith and running the race set before us with dedication, we must be the aggressor, the attacker. We must learn to do aggressive warfare that never gives up and never surrenders to sin. If we endure to the end, we will receive the crown of life.

This is not some victory wreath given to athletes who win a competition, nor is it some honor received here on earth. The crown of life is what we will receive after we have survived a life of trials, have overcome the pull of the ocean of sin, have learned to do offensive warfare that fights the good fight of faith, and runs the race set before us with perseverance because we love Christ above all else.

> *He that overcometh shall inherit all things; and I will be his God, and he shall be my son. (Revelation 21:7)*

We do not inherit all things unless we have overcome self, its affinity to sin, and have adhered faithfully to Christ Jesus as Lord and Savior. If we are to inherit all things, we must deny self and choose to follow Jesus by taking up our cross daily. We must comprehend the kingdom of God is taken by force (strength and energy). It is not given to us unless we have overcome (surmount and conquer) this life of sin by faith. We cannot conquer sin unless we have learned to be the warrior who is proficient in aggressive warfare.

It will only be achieved if we stay on the straight and narrow way that leads to life (Heaven). If we meander unto the broad and wide way that leads to death (Hell), we will not overcome and inherit all things. God will not be our Father, and we will not be his child. There is no inheritance without overcoming.

God's soldiers must turn away from itching ear preachers teaching we can live in sin and possess eternal life. I am not saying we will not sin, but we will be convicted by the Holy Spirit and repent. We cannot indulge in a life of sin and believe a sinner's prayer absolves us from our sinful life. Jesus did not die that brutal death to free us from sin for us to continue in sin once we accept him as savior. As He overcame, we are to do likewise if we expect to inherit all things.

Inheriting all things should be the pursuit of all God's soldiers. We are not in this war for accolades or rewards in this life that will all perish. Our goal is to prevail through all we encounter no matter how arduous upon our flesh. We must have our attention focused upon our eternal inheritance.

With the reality of the arduous journey to Heaven, we are now armed with the knowledge of the necessity of self-denial. This war is not won by compromise, concession, or surrender to sin. Only the aggressor, the attacker, the fighter, the warrior who comprehends the importance of aggressive warfare will overcome and inherit all things.

> *Therefore, my beloved brethren, be ye stedfast, unmoveable, always abounding in the work of the Lord, forasmuch as ye know that your labour is not in vain in the Lord. (1 Corinthians 15:58)*

The apostle is encouraging us to keep fighting and keep running although we may feel we are getting nowhere. We may not always see results, but whatever we do for the Lord is not in vain. After all, the fight is not over until we have finished the fight. The race is not done until we have crossed the finish line.

> *9)And he said unto me, My grace is sufficient for thee: for my strength is made perfect in weakness. Most gladly therefore will I rather glory in my infirmities, that the power of Christ may rest upon me. 10)Therefore I take pleasure in infirmities, in reproaches, in necessities, in persecutions, in distresses for Christ's sake: for when I am weak, then am I strong. (2 Corinthians 12:9–10)*

Some may be thinking our life is too much. We have been fighting and fighting for years with this and there is no end. There is no way we can continue to do what God expects. That, soldier, is a lie from the devil who wants us to quit. He knows if we quit, there is no overcoming. If there is no overcoming, we will not inherit all things. If life was easy, there would be nothing to overcome.

We can count upon God's promise that his grace is sufficient for whatever suffering, whatever infirmity, whatever sin, whatever reproach, whatever persecution, whatever grief, whatever distress we may face in this life. If God calls us to do something, He gives us the grace to complete it. If God calls us to go through something, He gives us the grace to endure it. His grace enables his strength to be made perfect in our weakness. His grace empowers us to overcome all things.

God promises that the inheriting all things awaits all who fight the good fight of faith and run the race set before us with patience. We are not fighting or running in vain. We are focused not upon the fight or the race, but upon the goal of receiving our eternal inheritance with Christ. Because we keep our eyes upon the goal, we are encouraged to wage aggressive warfare against whatever may attempt to distract us from fighting or running.

> *But without faith it is impossible to please him: for he that cometh to God must believe that he is, and that he is a rewarder of them that diligently seek him. (Hebrews 11:6)*

God will respond to us and reward us when we sincerely look to him in faith. Our greatest reward will be our inheriting all things at the end of a life of steadfast and unmoveable faith in Christ.

Because we know God is a rewarder of those who diligently seek him, we must never tire of fighting or running. As God's soldiers, we must learn to be the aggressor, the seizer, taking authority over any sinful desires or any distraction trying to overtake us. We must always engage in aggressive warfare and call the plays through the Word of God. As we aggressively move forward, we will fight the good fight of faith and run the race set before us with persistence until we receive our eternal inheritance!

www.ingramcontent.com/pod-product-compliance
Lightning Source LLC
Chambersburg PA
CBHW071159090426
42736CB00012B/2384